HOW TO KNOW GOD'S VOICE
IN INTIMATE FRIENDSHIP

STUDY GUIDE

Lesson 8   **FEAR OF THE LORD**
   Scripture: **1 Kings 18 and 19**
   Dawson: Chapter 15
   Assigned Article: *"Beholding Him"* B. Bright

Lesson 9   **TOUCH NOT!**
   Scripture: **Numbers 11:1; 12:1–16**
   Dawson: Chapters 13 and 14
   Assigned Articles: *"I Saw The Lord"* M. Rutland
                     "The Power Of Words" G. Getz

Lesson 10 **SACRIFICING YOUR ISAAC**
   Scripture: **Genesis 14:18–24; 15:1–6; 22:1–19**
   Dawson: Chapter 16
   Assigned Articles: *"Sacrificing Your Isaac"* D.G. Lindsay
                     "Sacrifice Or Worship" P. Schoch

Lesson 11 **REWARDS OF FEARING THE LORD**
   Scripture: **1 Kings 2 and 3**
   Dawson: Chapters 17 and 18
   Assigned Articles: *"God's Righteousness: Our Only Basis For Ministry"* J. Cornwall
                     "Keeping Company With God" M. Lucado

Lesson 12 **COMMITMENT**
   Scripture: **2 Chronicles 16:9; 2 Kings 22:1 through 23:1-30**
   Dawson: Pages 179–186
   Assigned Articles: *"The Master's Choice"* C. Baker
                     "Wanted: Commitment Keepers" J. Ryan
                     "He Wants To Be With Me" S. Clark

Study Materials:

1. Bible, any version
2. Dawson, Joy, *Intimate Friendship with God,* Chosen Books, div. of Baker Publishing Group, P.O. Box 6287, Grand Rapids, MI 49516, www.chosenbooks.com, © 1986, 2008.
3. Various articles in the Study Guide
   a. Class Article—to be read in class
   b. Assigned Article—to be read in preparation for class

enjoy each other where our lives touch, even to the point of sharing common interests together; but we remain only at the first level.

Although the Scripture acknowledges that level of friendship, it speaks of something more: lovingkindness. The word is variously translated in the Scripture as "mercy, kindness, loyalty, or covenant love." It is a love loyalty based on blood covenant. When two parties entered into a blood covenant, the relationship between them was termed "lovingkindness." It meant that they could expect of each other and of themselves that the terms of the covenant would be honored.

In Christ, we are in a blood covenant relationship with the Father and with all of His children. The expected relationship between each believer and God, as well as with his brothers and sisters in Christ, is that of lovingkindness. It is the most difficult part of the outworking of the life of Christ — and usually the last to be flowed in spontaneously.

The essence of the world is involvement with oneself; we do not really notice others. The world goes to its parties wearing the masks that make sure no one knows who we really are. Religion has perfected mask wearing! So-called friendships are ships that pass in the night and generally do not even signal. If they do, sometimes it is with false information! When we come to Christ, it is a shock to be introduced to more than being available, but to a loyal covenant love that demands the giving of ourselves to another party. Paul describes this kind of love loyalty in his epistles.

And be kind to one another, tenderhearted, forgiving each other, just as God in Christ also has forgiven you. (Ephesians 4:32)

Bearing with one another, and forgiving each other, whoever has a complaint against anyone; just as the Lord forgave you, so also should you. (Colossians 3:13)

His love has been shed abroad in our hearts, and so we can live the kind of life that Paul is setting forth here. How do we work it out? How does the loyal love of God actually become actualized on a day-to-day basis? It can be easily stated in certain attitudes that must be present for loyalty to grow into the motivating power of our lives.

1. We recognize in each other the fact that we are both in the process of discovering who Christ is in us; we are babes on the way to maturity. When you stumble and fail, loyalty demands that I accept you knowing that I, too, fail in my onward walk with God.

However, understand the acceptance that we have for the other. It is not the careless acceptance that laughs at sin and says that anything goes. I will take your failure as seriously as God does, and as seriously as I believe you will take mine. In the light of the finished work of Christ I will forgive you, even as I have been forgiven and expect to be forgiven in future failures. Being loyal to you, I dare not stop at forgiveness, but expect to be a part of the restoration process in your life, bringing you back to a dynamic walk with God.

If your wrong affects me personally, I promise that I will not hold it as a grudge, letting it smolder until it is bitterness and malice inside of me. Loyal love demands that I share with you the wrong you are doing to me so that it can be worked out in love between us.

One thing loyal love promises: your failures will never be aired and discussed with anyone—not even the members of the prayer group. If I have to share you as a prayer request, I will simply mention your name; God knows all that is wrong. So many prayer groups should be renamed as "gossip groups!" Their prayer requests are nothing but sharing the gory details of another brother's problems.

DISLOYALTY IS NOT ALWAYS IN THE WORDS SPOKEN, BUT ALSO IN THE UNSPOKEN WORDS!

When you have shared your heart with me, you can rest assured that it is held as a sacred trust.

2. When you are broken in spirit and you are weeping on the inside, the one who is your loyal love friend will not gloat over you, but will be there for you. Lovingkindness does not always know what to say, but it will always be there to sit beside you.

Isaiah 32:1, 2 describes the mature person operating in Christ's love:

"Behold, a king will reign righteously, and princes will rule justly. And each will be like a refuge from the wind, And a shelter from the storm, Like streams of water in a dry country, Like the shade of a huge rock in a parched land."

The king who reigns is Jesus, but you and I are the princes; and it is given to us in Christ, and He in and through us, to be the refuge, shelter, stream of living water to the brother or sister who is broken. That is loyal friendship in a sentence.

3. Being loyal means that I do not allow myself to be sour when you prosper more than I do. You may have greater spiritual gifts than I and may be used of God more than I, but loyalty rejoices, putting aside any envious anger that might rise

you thought was a loyal brother or sister? If so, what do you do now?

1. If you have been disloyal, ask God's forgiveness. If the one you betrayed knows about it, ask his forgiveness, too. Among all the sins of mankind, there is none more wretched than disloyalty; in disloyalty we are being as unlike Him as we possibly could be.

2. If others have been disloyal to you, forgive them whether they ask for it or not. That is how He has forgiven us! Friendship resumes when they choose to accept the forgiveness. Do not despair of those you thought were your covenant friends who walked away in the day of your trouble.

Peter and John, who let Him down more than any of the others for they were the closest, ended up being His most loyal of all men on earth. *Part of their loyalty was in realizing just how disloyal they had been.*

In it all, Jesus remained loyal to them. It was as if He said, "I know you don't know what I mean by loyal love; but I continue to love you with a love you do not deserve, and soon you will begin to walk in it."

3. Realize that these times of hurting are in His hand. Out of it can come true friends that are not only available in times of trouble, but lovingkindness friends tested by the days of adversity.

Let the Spirit deal with you in this article. Your friends who have hurt you stand before God for themselves. Let the Holy Spirit search you to see any acts of disloyalty—and know that He who is in you not only cleanses from sin but is the power to be in you and through you the infinite love of God.

—Malcolm Smith describes himself as an evangelist to the evangelized, teaching believers who they are in Christ, the beloved of God and His dwelling place through the Spirit. He directs a non-residential Bible School and travels throughout the U.S., conducting retreats and meetings in churches and organizations of all denominations

Reprinted by permission: Covenant Love

they appear to us. Often He will show them to us mapped out in His Word.

Or He may tell us to ask directions from "fellow travelers"—those trustworthy Christians who know the old paths well. That was a crucial point for me.

I discovered no one travels the old paths alone; spiritual growth occurs in the midst of loving Christian fellowship.

Walk in the good way. Before I stopped to listen for God's direction, I tried to bring things about on my own—with God's help. But the good way means first seeing the path His Holy Spirit takes and then walking in it with Him. When we do, we receive the rest for our souls that He promised.

Rediscovering the old paths of the Holy Spirit has been the turning point of my life and ministry. Since that day two years ago, lives have been changed, people have been healed and God is being glorified. Our church has doubled to 4,000, and our crusades have filled stadiums in Buenos Aires with 60,000 people.

Perhaps you too are at a turning point, suffering through a spiritually dry period, struggling in ministry or just feeling something is missing. Has the Holy Spirit led you to a crossroad? If so, "Stand... and see, and ask...where the good way is, and walk in it; then you will find rest for your souls."

—Claudio Freidzon was born near Buenos Aires, Argentina in 1955. In 1986 he founded the King of Kings Church in Argentina. Claudio Freidzon is also the best selling author of "Holy Spirit, I Hunger For You!" and "From Glory To Glory."

Reprinted by permission: Charisma Magazine and Strang Communications Company.

to urge me forward, excite my heart and deepen my worship.

Mary, the mother of Jesus, knew what it was to have such whisperings of the Spirit and to hold them to herself: *But Mary treasured up all these things, pondering them in her heart* (Luke 2:19).

These shared intimacies do not take place in the crowd. God knows it requires stillness, where He can speak without our restless hearts interrupting. That is why He calls us into the secret place alone.

///

SILENCE IS NOT THE WORLD EMPTIED OF SOUND. IT IS TO HAVE YOUR WORLD FILLED WITH THE STILLNESS AND HUSH OF HIS PRESENCE.

///

I once went alone to an idyllic spot down by a river, where it was so peaceful and quiet away from the crowds. I lay in the grass, my back warmed by the earth that had drunk from the sun shining down through the trees. Apart from the occasional bee buzzing in the clover, the air was still. It carried the sound of running waters tumbling over stones as they raced towards the waterfall below. I thought of His voice which, like the sound of many waters, had so frequently broken through the clamor all around and hushed my restless soul.

Silence is not the world emptied of sound. It is to have your world filled with the stillness and hush of His presence. Speech would be an unwelcome intruder in the God-filled secret place. It is not that you have run out of things to say to Him. It is simply that, at this moment, silence is your most eloquent form of speech.

Like a river, our worship can tumble or run still. It is not that some people worship this way and others that way, according to their personality. That would mean worship was governed by our natural temperament. No, it is *spirit and truth*. People's moods change—sometimes mellow, reflective, sober; at other times happy, extravagant, joyful. But every mood is an opportunity to express our worship. We worship Him, not according to a stereotyped personality pattern, but in the spontaneity of the Spirit in every wholesome mood of life.

Sometimes, after listening to the car radio or a tape for some hours during a long journey, I switch it off and suddenly realize the silence again. It is often here in the worship-filled silence that God's secrets are shared with us.

This silence is not the emptiness of soul but the stillness of the inner being. Gone now are the rushing thoughts, the clashing senses, the active mind urging us to do something, the protesting priorities clamoring for attention. Here in His presence we have come to rest.

Be still, and know that I am God: I will be exalted among the nations, I will be exalted in the earth (Psalm 46:10). Stillness does not come easy in the contemporary world where we are trained to assert ourselves to tackle our responsibilities. To efficient and diligent persons, the thought of leaving the situation, of not *doing something*, is anathema. But with God, to be still is a great strength.

Moses discovered this in the great exodus of Israel from Egypt: *But Moses said to the people, "Do not fear! Stand by and see the salvation of the Lord which He will accomplish for you today; for the Egyptians whom you have seen today, you will never see them again forever. The Lord will fight for you while you keep silent"* (Ex. 14:13,14).

It is in such times of seeming inactivity that we realize God is most active on our behalf. When we are the most quiet, His is the only sound to be heard—whispering the secret counsels of His heart and mind to us.

Possibly the question we most need to ask ourselves is not, "Can we trust God with our secret longings and desires?" but, "Can He trust us with His?"

—Bryn Jones has served as a pastor, teacher, author and editor in the U. S. and the U.K. He founded the International Christian Leadership Programme, Help International (a humanitarian relief and development agency) and The Institute of World Concerns, a research institute for the serious study of world peace through the application of biblical principles. Jones has written numerous books, including The Radical Church.

Reprinted with permission: Psalmist Magazine

your God, by obeying His voice, and by holding fast to Him. (Deuteronomy 30: 19, 20)

Joshua testified:
    …choose for yourselves today whom you will serve…as for me and my house we will serve the Lord. (Joshua 24:15)

Elijah called on the people to choose:
    …How long will you hesitate between two opinions? If the Lord is God, follow Him; but if Baal, follow him. (1 Kings 18:21)

The presence of the tree of the knowledge of good and evil in the Garden of Eden tells us plainly that for man to be the person God made him, he must make choices. Exodus 19:5 tells how God said that the Israelites would be His special people if they obeyed His Word. The blessings of Deuteronomy 28 were contingent on the choices Israel made.

Jesus made it perfectly clear in John 14:23:
    …If anyone loves Me he will keep My word…

I AM A PERSON IN WHOM CHRIST LIVES BY HIS SPIRIT.

But the exertion of my will is not willpower! Willpower and positive thinking release power to change many situations. But they are in the category of our being the masters of our own lives. They do not bring us any closer to God than we were before.

The Gospel does not call us to change for the sake of changing! It calls us to become aligned to God's life in Christ—His love, wisdom and way of life. In Him we do not keep a list of rules, but enter into a life-changing relationship.

The Gospel is not an exercise of willpower, but the harnessing of our will to His power and life. The rest that the believer knows is not, "All of Him and none of me," but the result of a deliberate choice to let Him be our life. We are not in the bleachers watching Him play the game of our life! We play the game of life with Him, choosing in each and every situation that He is our Lord and our Life.

Looking at my problem, I affirm the truth; I am no longer a slave of Satan, but a child of God. I am a person in whom Christ lives by His Spirit. No longer a slave, I am free to choose the way my life will take.

In Christ we are now free! Chris does not have to lose his temper or hold grudges, and no believer needs to be chained to a habit. But God does not do it for us while we watch; our choices must be involved making us mature lovers of God, not robots.

We choose, as the free sons of God that we are, to put off the negative and put on the positive – the life of Christ. The choice is a total committal; the joining of our will to His will and strength. Chris says and means, "I am putting off anger and rage, and putting on the patience and meekness of Christ; not in the strength of my will, but in the strength of Him who lives within me."

We are not experimenting! It is not, "Well, I will see if it works!" That attitude actually hinders the work of God in our lives. Obviously, nothing will happen from such an attitude, and the next time God challenges our faith we have a history of failure that sides with doubt.

The man in Christ says, "I know Christ in me is willing that I stop this course of action—this habit or lifestyle—and begin to live His life. From this day forward I am going to will His will. I am choosing every day that His life and strength are mine in this specific area."

This does not mean we have no more temptation in that area. The born again drug addict is tempted to get a drug high. The alcoholic in Christ still has calls to enter into alcoholic euphoria. Chris is going to be tempted to rage at any situation that crosses what he wants.

… IN (HIS) STRENGTH I AM NOW CHOOSING TO ACT.

To these temptations we do not respond with willpower saying, "I won't, I won't!" Rather, we state, "I recognize that Christ is my life, and in that strength I am now choosing to act." Instead of giving in to the temptation, we act as if Christ is our life.

As we act, we discover life, power and strength that is beyond ourselves. We live in that we choose His life, but He lives in that it is His life at the source of our actions. It is not willpower, but our choosing to live by His power.

The fact that the believer wants to renounce the negative and live in the positive comes from God. Philippians 2:13 tells us that God not only is the strength to do His will in us, but He is the originator of His will in us. In us "it is God who is at work…to will and to work for His good pleasure."

The Spirit does not put His desire in us to tease us, but it

it's always to complain or beg.

I felt tears forming and sat back down on my rough pew. The words of an old song came to mind.

*My God and I go through the fields
together.
We walk and talk as good friends
should and do.
We clasp our hands, our voices ring
with laughter.
My God and I walk through the
meadow's hue.*

My life, it seems, is filled with "kitchen things"—fixing food for others. That morning, however, I understood what Jesus meant when He said to Martha, "Mary has chosen what is better." Nothing is as important as wasting time with God.

—Jamie Buckingham devoted his talents and sacrificed his time to teach and spread the gospel, eventually becoming an internationally renowned author, columnist, and conference speaker. He was a friend to nearly every significant Christian leader in the charismatic movement until his death in 1992 at the age of 59.

Reprinted by permission: Charisma Magazine and Strang Communications Company.

April 1991, Charisma

voice! I believe in spiritual warfare, but true spiritual authority comes from knowing and seeking the face of God. *Those who know their God will display strength and do great exploits (Dan. 11:32)*. Not those who know all the right words or have a mental understanding of God.

CALL THE SOLEMN ASSEMBLY!

God is ultimately going to fulfill His word, and He's given us the privilege of participating in that fulfillment. Before every major revival the Spirit has always moved on the hearts of His people to begin to fast and pray!

In the Old Testament the English word "congregation" is the translation of several Hebrew words that mean "an appointed meeting" or "an assembly called together", "a sacred assembly gathered by God and appointed to be His covenant people." In this passage of Joel the Lord is calling the whole assembly of the congregation of Israel.

A Hebrew belonged, at the most basic level, to a house, then to a family (a collection of houses), then to a tribe (a collection of families), and then to the congregation (a collection of tribes).

Imagine if we as individual Christians would respond to this trumpet and set aside times of fasting and praying. Getting away by ourselves to be alone with God not just for 30 minutes but for one, two or three days! Then, as entire families, we set aside days of fasting and prayer. Can you imagine the results of families fasting and praying together? Restoration of marriages, the turning of the hearts of the parents to the children and the children to the parents.

What if an entire church set aside a weekend to gather to fast and pray. Mingling worship and intercession. Singing those interces-

sory judgments against the enemy, as the Priests and Prophets did throughout the Old Testament (Example: Ps.7 and 68). Putting everything on hold, even the weddings, Joel said! A Saturday and Sunday given to prayer and fasting by the whole assembly, even the little ones! (The little ones may not be able to fast, but they will sure learn something by observing their parents taking their God seriously.)

If every church that calls on the name of Jesus in a city set aside a Saturday and Sunday to come before God with weeping and mourning over their sins and the sins of their city, crying out for God's mercy and release of His Spirit, I believe God would move heaven and earth on behalf of this kind of unified prayer!

We would begin to see His answer in Joel 2:28-32 (NIV) . . . *and afterward, I will pour out my Spirit on all people. Your sons and daughters will prophesy* . . . I believe some of the first stirrings of the Spirit are going to be among the youth. If the young people of this generation do not experience the manifest power of God in their lives, we will lose many of them to the attractions of the world!

Unfortunately God's timetable is different than ours. We want instant answers to all our prayers, and many times lack the perseverance to keep praying if we don't see the answers right away. We must maintain a long-range vision for God's purposes and get on board for the long haul.

THE FORK IN THE ROAD

Our human tendency is to be like Abraham and Sarah who grew weary of waiting for the promised child and chose to look about them and copy what had become an accepted practice of the

day to produce life. The result was an Ishmael! To obey is better than sacrifice! Don't try to copy other churches or ministries that seem to be successful. Abraham succeeded in bringing a son into the world, but his success in the short run has produced strife and sadness for thousands of years even to this present day!

We must stop looking for quick solutions for the church's problems and fix our eyes upon our Redeemer.

In the first two chapters of 1 Samuel we find the events leading up to the birth of the prophet Samuel and see God's divine plan for birthing His purposes in the Church. Hannah was barren unable to conceive year after year. Her rival Peninnah would provoke and vex her because of her barrenness! Interestingly, it states that God had closed her womb. How often have we felt barren and fruitless! The enemy loves to accuse and belittle us in our season of barrenness, driving us to seek after the newest fad or method, desperately trying to produce life! Hannah did not follow Sarah's example. Instead, she followed Joel's principle, pouring out her soul to God with weeping and fasting, until she conceived something from God's hand.

Read the prayer of thanksgiving of this godly and wise woman in 1 Sam. 2:1-10, as she states that it is God who lifts the needy and seats them with princes! Not our human schemes or ideas!

BUCKLE YOUR SEAT BELTS

We are living in a day of great change. The charismatic move is over and God is ready to birth something new and powerful in the Church. The period immediately before the giving birth is called "transition." It is the most

fear, force, guilt trips or manipulation—may seem to obtain quick results, but the fruits won't last. Even spiritual disciplines such as prayer, fasting, Bible study and witnessing often result in legalism, pride, insecurity or morbid introspection if pursued with the wrong motivation.

Christians will sometimes move into action faster if they are told God is angry at them, or that they will fail miserably and lose everything that's dear to them on earth if they don't get busy performing and producing. But in the long run, many sincere believers wind up damaged, discouraged and burned out if they build their spiritual lives on such a faulty foundation.

On the other hand, Christians who are rooted and grounded in the strong, secure love of God find deep and lasting motivation toward greater consistency, spiritual passion and maturity. As we begin to understand the Father's affection for us and the price Jesus paid to redeem us, our hearts melt with devotion and gratitude. We long for a fuller, more intimate knowledge of God—for heart-to-heart fellowship with Him.

As Paul explained to the Roman believers, "You have not received a spirit of slavery leading to fear again, but you have received a spirit of adoption as sons by which we cry out, 'Abba! Father!'" (Rom. 8:15, NASB).

SETTING YOUR HEART ON GOD

When we set our hearts to seek the Lord—when we decide to pursue *Him* more than we pursue other good things such as anointing, happiness and success—our lives begin to change in many ways. For example:

1. A focus on intimacy cleanses our spirits.

Jesus loved the church and *October 1995, Charisma*

gave Himself up for her "that He might sanctify her, having cleansed her by the washing of water with the word" (Eph. 5:26).

Just as you or I need a daily physical bath, we also need a daily spiritual bath. Accumulated "grime" and defilement lead to spiritual dullness. Inner corruption such as anger, slander, impatience and sensuality grieves the Holy Spirit and makes our spirits insensitive and unable to respond fully to Him. When we fix our hearts on the *person* of Jesus and dialogue with Him, however, the Word of God washes our spirits.

Of course, the accumulation of information about the Scriptures and the mental discipline of hours of Bible study will never thoroughly cleanse the inner man in the way that devotional, worshipful meditation upon God's Word will. In Bible study alone, we store up important scriptural facts and concepts. But when that study leads into personal dialogue with Jesus, we also experience growth in spiritual hunger, sensitivity and nearness to Him.

2. A focus on intimacy protects our souls.

We will never possess true purity without inward affection for Jesus. The person of Christ—not rules and regulations—guards our souls. External disciplines and standards of holiness without devotion for Jesus have very little real power or life in them.

Affection for Him, on the other hand, creates a hindrance to the temptations that plague us. It's not a matter of being afraid we might get caught. It's not an issue of fear that we might be shamed and lose honor, position, privileges or even the anointing. We have higher motives for resisting temptation than a fear of AIDS or of coming under divine discipline.

Our hearts are shielded by

our love and reverence for Christ. We are like newlyweds who are so aware of the love they share with one another that the temptation to have an affair with someone else seems absurd.

3. A focus on intimacy motivates our hearts.

When we are sowing to the Spirit (see Gal. 6:8), we are exposing ourselves to the presence of God whether we feel it or not. As focusing upon Him becomes the habit of our souls, we receive the wonderful anointing spoken of in Hebrews, "Who make His ... ministers a flame of fire" (Heb. 1:7). The flaming heart of Christ ignites our hearts. Fire begets fire.

I love the verse from the Song of Solomon where the beloved speaks to his bride and says, "Put me like a seal over your heart, like a seal on your arm. For love is as strong as death, jealousy is as severe as Sheol; its flashes are flashes of fire, the very flame of the Lord" (Song 8:6).

The holy flame of God is relentless and consuming. It will ignite a focused soul and release deep emotions of hunger for Jesus. However, if we are too busy, easily offended, bitter or self-absorbed, the flame will be diminished.

I'm not talking about diminishing the flame of God's love and affection for us. That never changes. Rather I'm talking about our passion and zeal for Him. We can lose our passion for Jesus without losing God's love for us; but a heart focused on intimacy will be motivated to pursue Him more.

4. A focus on intimacy satisfies our human spirits.

Intimacy with Christ satisfies the deep longing in our spirits. Though the Holy Spirit may give spiritual gifts to believers, and though we may derive some fulfillment from being effective in ministry, these things ultimately will not

Holiness' (Is. 35:8) to bring glory to his name."

THE PROCESS OF HOLINESS

Just as he who called you is holy, so be holy in all you do; for it is written: 'Be holy, because I am holy' " (1 Pe 1: 15-16). For years Christians have read this passage and then looked up with an expression befitting the Book of Lamentations.

Some have tried (unsuccessfully) to become holy by teeth-gritting determination, striving in the flesh to conquer sin.

Others have gone the route of creating and enforcing rigid sets of rules—"don't do this; don't go there" only to see their lives degenerate into ascetic legalism. Colossians 2:20-23 dismisses these "human commands" as being completely inadequate for Christian living.

Still others have compromised Christian character and brought reproach on Christ's name by rationalizing sinful habits. Declaring themselves "eternally secure," they have discredited the high calling to holy living as some antiquated, mystical state, quite unattractive and unattainable this side of eternity.

But today multitudes are gaining a revelation of the "splendor of his holiness" (Ps 96:9). On one side is a *positional holiness*. This is our instantaneous, holy, righteous standing before a holy God that is our gift when we trust in Jesus Christ. The other side is *progressive holiness*. This is God's working in us "his good purpose" (Php 2:13), to conform to the character of Christ.

How can we actively cooperate with him in the process? Hebrews 12:14 tells us: "Make every effort to live in peace with all men and to be holy; without holiness no one will see the Lord." This suggests three thoughts.

First, Spirit-led effort is required to become holy. Though no one can attain holiness apart from God's initiative and power working in his life, neither will he attain it without effort on his part. ("Letting go and letting God" is just another excuse for passivity!) "For the grace of God that brings salvation has appeared to all men. It teaches us to say 'No' to ungodliness and worldly passions, and to live self-controlled, upright and godly lives in this present age" (Tit 2:11-12).

Secondly, holiness is a lifelong process. It's the adventure of cooperating with the Holy Spirit as he both sanctifies us by the Word of God and transforms us by our willing obedience. "Sanctify them by the truth; your word is truth" (Jn 17:17).

Finally, the writer of Hebrews issues a solemn warning to those who might minimize holiness: "Without holiness no one will see the Lord." The more we become preoccupied with Jesus and his Word, loving and worshipping him and wanting to please him, the more we want to be holy.

"BUT I ALWAYS FAIL"

But how can I gain the victory over those areas where I repeatedly fall?

It is in these areas where we can most feel the awful sense of hopelessness caused by sin's power. Satan capitalizes on these by vicious whisperings: "Overcoming *this* sin is impossible. It's proof that you'll never live holy."

While it is true that in ourselves we cannot live a holy, overcomer's life, God has made provision for our holiness if we'll walk in faith and humble dependence upon him. Jesus came both to forgive *and* to liberate us from sin's power.

RELIGION, WITH ITS LIST OF "DOS AND DON'TS," MAY CHANGE OUR OUTWARD APPEARANCE, BUT IT NEVER CHANGES THE HEART.

Paul's "Declaration of Independence From Sin's Power" in Romans six exhorts us to personal holiness by: (1) *remembering* the old nature has been crucified (6:6); (2) *reckoning* ourselves dead to sin but alive to God (6:11)—believing we are no longer sin's slave but united to God who strengthens us; (3) *resisting* the temptation to yield our members to sin (6:12-13); and (4) *offering* our members as instruments of righteousness unto God (6:13), which leads to holiness (6:19).

What Paul is saying here is vital for us to grasp: *As a Christian I have the opportunity to sin but not the obligation!*

As a new Christian I wrote a paraphrase of Romans 6:6-7 on my hallway mirror: "I don't have to serve sin today, for I have been set free!" I'd confess it daily. After a few months, the reality of this verse hit me as my mind was renewed to believe this as more than a promise of future dreams fulfilled. I grasped it as a fact from the Word of God.

NAVIGATING THE GRAY AREAS

God's Word gives us helpful principles that we can apply to "gray areas." Asking ourselves the following questions could save us from plunging into trouble later on.

1. Is it beneficial—spiritually, mentally, and physically—to me as a Christian? (1 Co 6:12)
2. Can I do it in fullness of faith? (Ro 14:23) If I doubt, better do without!
3. Will it enslave me and bring me under its power? (1 Co 6:12)
4. Does it glorify God? (1 Co 10:31)
5. Is it good stewardship of time and/or money? (1 Co 4:2)
6. Will it dull my spirit and cause me to lose my edge in God? (Mt 5:8)
7. Will it grieve (sadden) the Holy Spirit? (Eph 4:30)
8. Will it edify others—does it seek their good? (1 Co 10:33)
9. Is it worth imitating? (1 Co 11:1)
10. Can it cause others to stumble? (Ro 14:21)

—Larry Tomczak has been involved in establishing and overseeing churches. He is an internationally known leader who has spoken on national TV broadcasts, to NFL and NBA teams and audiences of tens of thousands. Tomczak is the author of eight books including Divine Appointments: Making Every Day a Masterpiece and Clap Your Hands. He has been married for over thirty-five years and has four grown children.

Reprinted from Sovereign Grace Ministries (formerly People of Destiny), 7505 Muncaster Mill Rd., Gaithersburg, MD 20877. Used by Permission.

men throughout history—the first, literal Adam, and the second Adam, which is Jesus.

All of humankind was wrapped up in the first Adam—and when he sinned, we all became sinners. Then Jesus came forth as a new man—and, through his reconciliation on the cross, all of humankind potentially became gathered up in him. Today God recognizes only this one man, Jesus—and he is holy.

Like Adam, apart from Christ's redemption of us, we can never be holy. No matter how long we live or how hard we try—no matter how many prayers we utter, how often we read the Bible, or how many lusts we conquer—we will never be perfectly holy. The Bible says if we haven't fulfilled all the law—if we've had even one evil thought—then we've missed the whole law. And we cannot be holy.

Jesus stands alone in perfect holiness. And if any person is ever to stand before the heavenly father and be received by him, that person must be in Christ. God won't recognize any other man. (Thankfully, that includes our "old man"—the dead sinner in us!) We stand before the father without any merits or claims of our own—but only the grace of Christ.

Every time we go to our secret closet, our prayer should be: "Lord, I have no plea but Christ. I have nothing to bring to you—no good words, no holiness of my own. I come to you only because I am in Christ. And I claim his holiness. I know I stand before you uncondemned, because I am in him!"

THIS ONE MAN, JESUS, WHO IS HOLY AND BLAMELESS, HAS A BODY—AND WE ARE THAT BODY!

"Ye are the body of Christ, and members in particular" (1 Corinthians 12:27). We are the very members of Christ's body! By faith, we are made bone of his bone and flesh of his flesh.

And now we all have been adopted into one family, as part of the one man: **"So we, being many, are one body in Christ, and every one members one of another"** (Romans 12:5).

You see, out of the grave came a new man. And from the time of the cross, all who repent and believe in this new man are gathered up in him: **"By one Spirit are we all baptized into one body, whether we be Jews or Gentiles, whether we be bound or free; and have been all made to drink into one Spirit. For the body is not one member, but many"** (1 Corinthians 12:13-14).

There is no longer any black, white, yellow, brown, Jew, Muslim or Gentile. We are all of one blood—one new man—in Christ Jesus!

And because of Christ's work on the cross, man could no longer attempt to be holy by keeping the law and the commandments. He couldn't become holy by good works, righteous deeds, human effort or strivings of the flesh:

"That he might reconcile both unto God in one body by the cross, having slain the enmity thereby" (Ephesians 2:16). **"Having abolished in his flesh the enmity, even the law of commandments contained in ordinances; for to make in himself of twain (two) one new man, so making peace"** (verse 15).

Only one man would be accepted by the father—the new, resurrected man! And when this new man presented to his father all who had faith in him, the father responded, "I receive you all as holy—because you are in my holy son!" **"…he hath made us accepted in the beloved"** (Ephesians 1:6).

Moreover, we have been sealed by the Holy Spirit: **"That in the dispensation of the fullness of times he might gather together in one all things in Christ…in whom also after that ye believed, ye were sealed with that Holy Spirit of promise"** (verses 10,13).

So, you see, holiness is not something we do, or attain, or work up. Rather, it is something we be_lieve_! God accepts us as holy only as we have faith in Christ and abide in him. The path to holiness is not through human ability, but through faith!

This is God's wonderful answer to the anxious cries of multitudes of Christians, who thirst for an understanding of how to be holy. We are holy only as we rest in Christ's holiness! Our holiness is his holiness—flowing to us, the branches, from the root.

Yet, at times, this biblical doctrine of holiness hasn't always been the practice of the church. Often holiness has been thought of only in terms of outward behavior.

My preacher grandfather is an example of this. He was a Nazarene minister in the early holiness movement, and he didn't allow Christians to wear feathers in their hats. He kept a little pair of gold scissors in his pocket—and whenever someone came to the altar and bowed her head, he would snip off any feathers!

Yet my grandfather chewed tobacco, because there was no "holiness prohibition" against it. He even kept a spittoon near him on the pulpit, so he could chew while he preached. He would turn his head and spit out the juice—all while preaching against women who wore lipstick!

I have heard holiness preachers rail for hours against women's makeup, certain types of dress, length of hair and other people into the desert, where there were no grocery stores, no malls, not even a well of water. He would have to depend wholly on God for everything!

You have to understand—Moses had already tried to act as a deliverer in the power of his flesh. Forty years before, he had taken sword in hand and killed a cruel Egyptian slave driver. And now God was saying, "Moses, your zeal has to be sanctified—or it will destroy you! Are you willing to put down your sword, and trust in my sword? Will you put off all hope of being a deliverer in your own power and ability? Will you put off all confidence in your flesh to do my will?

THE HOLINESS GOD DEMANDS IS UTTERLY ABOVE AND BEYOND ALL HUMAN POWER TO ACHIEVE!

It is impossible for any of us to achieve holiness in God's sight by our own strength or willpower. There is only one way to be holy—and one principle by which to approach the Lord in our Christian service. We must come to him saying, "Lord, I have nothing to give you. You have to do it all!"

You can be free of all lusts, of every evil desire, and still not be holy. You can be a wonderful person, a loving mate, an upright and honest person, and still not be holy. On the contrary, all of our human goodness is as filthy rags in God's sight!

Yet we remain convinced, "If I could just get victory over this one last, remaining sin, I'd be able to live holy." So we take sword in hand—the sword of willpower, promises, good intentions—and we set out to kill the enemy in our hearts, in an attempt to gain victory.

But it will never happen! We can never be holy while standing on the ground of self-righteousness. The shoes of flesh have to be put off!

Years ago, many evangelical churches sang a gospel song that I absolutely hated. It says, "Forgive me, Lord, and try me one more time." No—that is theologically incorrect! God would never put our eternal future at such a great risk. If our salvation depended on such trial and error, none of us would ever make it to heaven!

Beloved, you and I face the same burning bush Moses did. And that bush is a type of God's fiery zeal against all flesh brought into his presence masquerading as holiness. He says to us, "You can't stand before me on that kind of fleshly ground. There is only one holy ground—and that is faith in my son and his work on the cross!"

This is the only way God ever could have saved and reconciled a whole world. If our works merited our salvation, only a select number would be candidates for salvation. But I believe in the doctrine of unlimited atonement—that Christ died potentially for all of humankind.

Many of my favorite Puritan writers, such as John Owen, believed the opposite. Their doctrine taught that "election" means God has chosen certain people for his kingdom, and that all others are damned. But I personally do not believe this teaching is supported in scripture. On the contrary, I believe that through Jesus' work on the cross, the whole world is potentially reconciled to God. Anyone who hears his word, repents of sin, and turns to him in faith, becomes in him – a part and member of his body!

This means God can save even the worst of humankind. We can behold the worst thief, rapist, murderer, drug addict or alcoholic—people who have no good works at all—and testify, "By repentance and faith, they can be presented righteous in Christ Jesus!"

That is the true, saving power of God. Yet many Christians live as if their works are sufficient. On judgment day, they'll stand before God in their flesh, saying, "Look at everything I've done for you, Lord. I've striven to stay clean and holy. I've prophesied, fed the poor, healed the sick, cast out demons. And I've done it all to please you!"

But God will answer, "I never knew you—because you were never on the proper ground! You never took your shoes off, setting aside your confidence in the flesh."

"You didn't do any of these things through the power of my Spirit. You did them all in your own strength. And they are a stench in my nostrils! I accept the righteousness of only one man—my son. And I do not see my son in you. You are not in Christ!"

"Of him are ye in Christ Jesus, who of God is made unto us wisdom, and righteousness, and sanctification, and redemption: that, according as it is written, He that glorieth, let him glory in the Lord" (1 Corinthians 1:30-31). In other words: "I won't allow any human beings to glory in my presence. They will glorify me only through my son—who each day is becoming their wisdom, righteousness and holiness!"

THERE IS ONLY ONE GROUND UPON WHICH YOU CAN BE MADE HOLY— AND THAT IS TOTAL AND COMPLETE TRUST IN CHRIST!

When I speak of total trust in Christ, I mean not only trust in his saving power, but trust in his keeping power as well. We have to

comes not from attending how-to seminars, or hearing famous speakers, or absorbing self-improvement messages from books or tapes. No—it comes from having a revelation of God, period! And God has already given us that revelation of himself, in Exodus 34.

Seeing God's glory also changes our relationships with others. Paul tells the Ephesian church, **"You've seen and tasted the glory of God. Now, be a reflection of that glory to others!"** **"Be ye kind to one another, tenderhearted, forgiving one another, even as God for Christ's sake hath forgiven you"** (Ephesians 4:32).

Now let me speak to you about walking in the glory of God.

THE REVELATION OF GOD'S GLORY TO US HAS EVERYTHING TO DO WITH OUR COMMUNION WITH HIM.

Many Christians talk about intimacy with the Lord—walking with him, knowing him, having fellowship with him. But we can't have true communion with God unless we receive into our hearts the full revelation of his love, grace and mercy.

Communion with God consists of two things: 1) Receiving the love of the father, and 2) loving him in return. You can spend hours each day in prayer, telling the Lord how much you love him—but that isn't communion. If you haven't received his love, you haven't had communion with him. You simply can't share intimacy with the Lord unless you're secure in his love for you.

The psalmist encourages us to **"enter into (God's) gates with thanksgiving and into his courts with praise"** (Psalm 100:4). What's the reason for such praise

and thanksgiving? And why are we given such a bold invitation? It's because we're shown the kind of God we're to come to: **"For the Lord is good; his mercy is everlasting; and his truth endureth to all generations"** (verse 5).

I know when I come to my Lord, I'm not coming to a hard, fierce, demanding father. He doesn't wait for me with an angry countenance, anxious to put a rod to my back. He doesn't trail me, waiting for me to fail so he can say, "I caught you!"

No—I'm coming to a father who has revealed himself to me as pure, unconditional love. He's kind and tenderhearted, full of grace and mercy, anxious to lift all my cares and burdens. And I know he'll never turn me down when I call on him.

That's why I'm to come into his courts with praise and thanksgiving—because I'm thankful for who my God is. He cares about everything concerning me!

Few believers, however, have laid hold of God's love for them by faith. They live in fear and despair, with little or no hope, always facing a storm. They can't understand why their lives aren't fulfilled, why they're full of such turmoil and confusion. They often think, "I pray daily, and I read my Bible, I constantly show God how much I love him. So why don't I have rest and peace?"

It's because they've never grasped the truth that God loves them! They haven't comprehended that, in spite of all their weaknesses and failures, their heavenly father cares about everything they're going through!

TRUE LOVE IS MANIFESTED IN TWO THINGS: REST AND REJOICING.

The prophet Zephaniah says something incredible about God's love for us. He writes, **"The Lord thy God in the midst of thee is mighty; he will save, he will rejoice over thee with joy; he will rest in his love, he will joy over thee with singing"** (Zephaniah 3:17).

This verse tells us two important things about how the Lord loves us:
1. God rests in his love for his people.

In Hebrew, the phrase "he will rest in his love" reads, "He shall be silent because of his love." God is saying in essence, "I've found my true love, and I'm totally satisfied! I don't need to look elsewhere, because I have no complaint. I'm completely fulfilled in this relationship, and I won't take my love back. My love is a settled matter!"

Zephaniah is telling us, "This is God's love for you! He wants you to know, 'I've found what I'm looking for—and it's you! You bring great joy to me'"
2. God gets great pleasure from his people.

Zephaniah testifies, **"He rejoices over you with singing"** (see same verse). He's saying, in other words, "God's love for you is so great; it puts a song on his lips!"

To "rejoice" means to have joy and delight. It's an outward expression of internal delight. It's also the highest expression of love. The Hebrew word Zephaniah uses for "rejoice" here is "tripudiare"—meaning, "to leap, as one overcome with joyful ecstasy."

Can you conceive of your heavenly father being so in love with you that he leaps with joy at the very thought of you? Can you receive his word that he loved you before the world was created, before humankind existed, before you were even born? Can you accept that he loved you even after you fell

I become, he'll rescue me. He'll hover over me through it all, never allowing me to be crushed. He'll always be kind and tender to me!"

This is when true communion begins. We're to be convinced each day of God's unchanging love for us. And we're to show him we believe his revelation about himself. John writes, **"We have known and believed the love that God hath to us. God is love; and he that dwelleth in love dwelleth in God, and God in him"** (1 John 4:16).

This belief alone can heal your soul. It's your only weapon against the devil, who lies that you're too unworthy to pray or draw near to God. Convincing yourself of this truth is the only way to open yourself to true communion.

If you've ever been in love with someone, you know what I'm talking about. Imagine a husband who's away on business much of the time, but who's utterly in love with his wife. He calls his beloved spouse every night he's away. And from time to time he calls home just to leave a message for her on their answering machine. His message to her goes something like this:

"Hi honey. I'm calling to let you know that just the thought you're there, loving me, brings me strength. It's going to be the lift I need for the day. I know I'm going to have a tough time with work today. But I've just read the letter you wrote to me, and oh, what a joy! Just knowing you're thinking of me makes me overflow with ecstasy!"

That's the love the heavenly father has for you. Trust in it!

THE OTHER SIDE OF COMMUNION IS OUR LOVING GOD BACK!

Walking in God's glory means not only that we receive the father's love, but that we love him back as well. It's about mutual af-

fection—both giving and receiving love. The Bible tells us, **"...thou shalt love the Lord thy God with all thine heart, and with all thy soul, and with all thy might"** (Deuteronomy 6:5).

God says to us, **"My son, give me thine heart..."** (Proverbs 23:26). His love demands that we reciprocate—that we return to him a love that's total, undivided, requiring all our heart, soul, mind and strength.

However, the Lord tells us in no uncertain terms, "You can't earn my love. The love I give to you is unmerited!" John writes, **"Herein is love, not that we loved God, but that he loved us, and sent his Son to be the propitiation for our sins"** (1 John 4:10). **"We love him, because he first loved us"** (verse 19).

We didn't wake up one day, decide to walk away from our sins, and turn to Jesus. No—the Spirit of God reached down into the wilderness of our lives, showed us our lostness and made us miserable in our sin. He sent us his word to show us truth, sent his Spirit to convict us, and then came after us himself. He did it all for us.

And now, just as God's love for us is marked by rest and rejoicing, so our love for him must have these same two elements:

1. David expresses a rest in his love for God when he writes, **"Whom have I in heaven but thee? And there is none upon earth that I desire beside thee"** (Psalm 73:25). The heart that loves the Lord ceases completely from looking elsewhere for comfort. Rather, it finds full contentment in him. To such a lover, God's lovingkindness is better than life itself!

2. Such a heart also rejoices in its love for God. It sings and dances in joyous ecstasy over the Lord. When a child of God knows how much his father loves him, it puts a

delight in his soul!

The Bible also tells us that our love for the father must be conveyed through his son. Jesus says, **"...no man cometh unto the Father, but by me"** (John 14:6). It's by Christ alone that we're accepted by the father and have access to him.

Moreover, God placed all his goodness, love, mercy and grace—that is, his glory—in his son. And he sent Jesus to manifest and reveal that glory to us. Thus, Christ comes to us as the express image of our loving father. **"As the Father hath loved me, so have I loved you: continue ye in my love"** (John 15:9).

God loves us as we stand in Christ. And, in turn, we show love for God in our love for Jesus. As the head of the church, and as our high priest, Jesus carries our love to the father for us.

Now let me give you one of the most powerful verses in all of scripture. Proverbs gives us these prophetic words of Christ: **"Then I was by him, as one brought up with him; and I was daily his delight, rejoicing always before him; rejoicing in the habitable part of his earth; and my delights were with the sons of men"** (Proverbs 8:30-31).

Beloved, we're the sons being mentioned here! From the very foundations of the earth, God foresaw a body of believers joined to his son. And even then the father delighted and rejoiced in these sons. Jesus testifies, "I was my father's delight, the joy of his being. And now all who turn to me in faith are his delight as well!"

So, how do we love Jesus in return? John answers, **"This is the love of God, that we keep his commandments; and his commandments are not grievous"** (1 John 5:3).

And what are his command-

liberate action of turning to that "something right," we will again find ourselves face-to-face with that "something wrong." If all we do is try to turn away from something, we will keep coming back to it.

Digging deeper, I read that *repentance* also means "to fetch back home." Repenting is not just a turning around aimlessly at God's barked command, without direction, without any sense of welcome; rather, it is an invitation by God to turn our lives around and set our hearts back toward Him.

To *repent* can further be translated to mean "to convert" or "to exchange." In repentance, we take the currency of the world—thoughts, feelings, desires and actions in our lives which are wrong—and exchange them for the currency of God's kingdom in the same way we would travel to another country and convert our money for theirs. God offers us an exchange, a trade-in, not just a turning away.

In this way repentance ceases to be a difficult experience. Instead it becomes a wonderful way to get our lives set aright.

Repentance must start with conviction. Like so many other Christian words, "conviction" has been spiritualized to the point where its meaning hardly registers at all.

The prodigal son was convicted in his pig's sty—in the midst of the mess his sin caused. But he could not, nor can we, repent in the pig's sty. Repenting is the going home, realizing the contrast between where we have been living and where Father God wants us to live.

Repentance never makes excuses. It never blames others. We cannot repent of something we cannot openly admit we are doing, and we cannot repent of something we do not believe is *wrong*.

When God convicts or corrects us, He always does so in hope. That is, instead of focusing on what we have not done that we should have done or what we have not been that we should have been, godly conviction points to what we can start doing and start becoming. Conviction is good news; it says, "Here is one more detail in your life which you can 'exchange,' 'convert' or 'turn in' for another installment of life.

This is why we should welcome conviction as the psalmist did: "Search me, O God, and know my heart; try me and know my anxious thoughts; and see if there be any hurtful way in me, and lead me in the everlasting way" (Ps. 139:23-24).

Many people who claim they have been convicted have not really become convinced of their guilt, and they either lie or fool themselves. Some of the more common pseudo convictions people confuse with genuine conviction include:

"Poor Me"—People who say this want others to feel badly for them either because of the consequences they face as a result of their sin or because of how terribly difficult the situation was that pushed them in to the sin. The sin itself gets lost in the shuffle of self-pity.

True repentance is sorry only for the sin and asks for no sympathy for the sinner. God will grant mercy but not excuses or exceptions.

"Whoops"—Rather than coming openly and freely to confess, people who say this make full disclosure of their sin and demonstrate sorrow only *after* they have been found out. Once the sin they have been hiding is exposed, they regret it but know they would continue to have done it if they hadn't been caught. They are upset because they were not careful enough.

True repentance is eager to confess, and a repentant heart is grateful when its sins are found out.

"What About"—People under this false sense of conviction want to know when they will be off probation, when their ministry can resume and exactly what is expected of them during their restoration period so that they can get beyond this inconvenience of sin's consequences. They come wanting to negotiate a temporary contract which will limit their disadvantages while they are undergoing rehabilitation.

True repentance is so consumed with the awful fact of what it already knows (the sin committed) that it cares to know nothing except the wonderful fact of Jesus' sacrifice. True repentance sits selflessly silenced and humbled by God's love without trying to pin down an exact program or timing for restoration to ministry.

"Learned Lots"—You hear this mostly in people's testimonies of how they walked away from the Lord, lived in rebellion, enjoyed the pleasures of sin, then were finally restored back to God. Their conviction grows philosophical, and they try to convince themselves and others that they "learned a lot while away from God." Through some glib reading of Romans 8:28, they try to minimize the loss in their life through sin by marveling at how God can even use sin for His purposes.

True repentance sees no glory, no good, no advantage gained through sin. A truly repentant heart knows that, compared with all we might have learned while walking with the Lord in obedience, we learn nothing of eternal value nor do we produce any lasting fruit while walking away from the Lord in rebellion.

Isaiah 6:9-11 sheds further light on what real repentance is and why it seems so elusive for some people. God says a peculiar thing: "Render the hearts of this tual inheritance. Many people who never seem to make any progress in the way of the Lord—people who get saved and move on a bit, then get stuck in an eternal treadmill—are usually people who do not truly repent.

True repentance is demonstrated when we choose to put our complete trust in God. Mark 1:15 says, "Repent, and put your trust in the good news." We have not fully repented unless we willingly embrace whatever the Lord has for us and trust that His *way will* work.

As long as we leave room for other options—including giving up on God or trusting in our own way rather than His—then we have not repented. Repentance is not something we try for a while to see if it works. In repentance, we voluntarily give up our right to have other options. Thus, our hearts are truly repentant only when we so cling to the Lord and are so inclined to the Lord that He really is our *only* hope.

I discovered this principle working in my life. God alerted me to my selfish laziness in not helping Pamela. Many instances of past failure came to my mind. I was convicted and asked for forgiveness. As time went along, I became acutely aware of those selfish, slothful tendencies in the midst of what I was doing.

From there, God began to convict me of the fact that I would be prone to selfishness in the future—not just with Pamela and housework, but in other areas too. I had the option 1) to listen to the enemy and continue to sin because all of my past repenting seemingly hadn't worked or 2) to repent of what I had done and of what I would have done in the future. Only by repenting could I exchange my wrongness for His righteousness. That is what changes behavior.

Suddenly, the change that had been happening in my heart produced real change in my behavior and in the baby's diapers. My repentance was fruitful.

Since that victory over habitual laziness, I have eagerly applied fruitful repentance to many sins in my life. I have yet to find one that is immune to the process.

—Daniel A. Brown has served as one of the pastors at the Church on the Way and as a founder of The Coastlands in Aptos, California. He heads up Commended to The Word and travels the globe teaching leaders to "Love, mend, train and send people into more ministry than they would think to do on their own."

Reprinted by permission: Charisma Magazine and Strang Communications Company.

That day has arrived; the Lord has handed the bill of holiness to me; and he's instructed me to hand it to you too.

There are Christians running around today who are saying, "Oh, great. Jesus is coming!" But many of them don't realize that they aren't ready for his return. They don't understand that they will be standing before a *holy* Father, a *righteous* Judge. Their hearts aren't ready; their lives aren't ready; they've made no preparations; they haven't kept their vows. They have no fear of God.

AMOS

The nation of Israel was in a situation similar to ours when Amos prophesied back in the mid-eighth century B.C. During this time Israel was enjoying great prosperity, military victories, and political success. They were secure and smug, confident that God was pleased with them. They thought of themselves as the people of God, the *chosen ones*.

But they were deceived, for they also practiced idolatry, immorality, oppression of the poor, corruption, and materialism. Because of Israel's sin, God sent Amos to warn them of his impending judgment; he would unleash the full fury of the Assyrians from the North—crushing, capturing, and scattering Israel.

A BROTHER IN THE CHURCH PROPHESIED, "WE'RE RIDING ON SOMEONE ELSE'S CREDIT CARD."

Amos came saying, "Woe to you who long for the day of the Lord! Why do you long for the day of the Lord? That day will be darkness, not light" (Amos 5:18). They weren't prepared, so they will be surprised and disappointed. In scripture light symbolizes grace; darkness judgment. Israel, so confident of being blessed, would be judged severely and harshly. Their minds were dulled because they had never sought God, submitted to his word, or allowed him to deal with them.

They failed to recognize that God was sovereignly blessing them. Instead, they were lulled into spiritual passivity by their success and prosperity. They were so blind that they *welcomed* the day of the Lord, not recognizing how terrible his judgment for their sin would be.

LAODICEA

Like Israel, much of the Western church today is secure and smug, not recognizing our desperate condition and the impending judgment of God on our sin.

Confident of our riches and gifts, we act like the Laodicean church that the Lord rebuked in John's revelation:

You say, 'I am rich; I have acquired wealth and do not need a thing.' But you do not realize that you are wretched, pitiful, poor, blind and naked. I counsel you to buy from me gold refined in the fire, so you can become rich; and white clothes to wear, so you can cover your shameful nakedness; and salve to put on your eyes, so you can see (Rev. 3:17-18).

The Laodiceans took great pride in their financial wealth, textile industry, and a famous eye salve. God said they were in need of "gold" refined by the fires of testing and endurance, "white clothes" of purity, and "salve" to restore their eyesight.

The Laodiceans forgot God, and he rebuked them severely for it: "Those whom I love I rebuke and discipline. So be earnest and repent" (Rev. 3:19). I shudder each time I read this passage, receiving comfort only when I realize his rebuke and discipline come because he loves us.

An experience back in 1985 illustrated how, like the Laodiceans, the Anaheim Vineyard had drifted from the Lord and become "lukewarm" spiritually (Rev. 3:16). During the year I preached over 100 messages on prayer, but the church never received them. A few individuals did, and had they not, we wouldn't be here today. But most never even heard the word.

Sunday after Sunday I threw out the "seed" of personal prayer; the ground didn't take it. Nothing sprang up. I kept waiting for fruit. Then I sensed the Lord saying, "It's over."

I said, "But I don't see anything."

He said, "I don't either. But wait. It'll grow."

In our success we became smug and lost our passion for God. Our spiritual senses were so dulled that we couldn't hear him calling us to a higher plane of communion with him. But as he did with the Laodiceans, the Lord said, "Here I am! I stand at the door and knock. If anyone hears my voice and opens the door, I will come in and eat with him, and he with me" (Rev. 3:20). God has given us another chance to turn to him, because he is merciful and forgives our sins (Ps. 79:38-39).

MIXED OFFERINGS

A characteristic of pharisaic unrighteousness is an emphasis on the outward signs of religion—church attendance and public displays of "religion." Of course, usually this is nothing more than an attempt to assuage guilty consciences, to make us feel better about our sin.

ness and justice, with private purity and public equity. Then by his grace we will reign with him at the Father's side, never again to leave God's presence (Rev. 3:12, 21).

—John Wimber was a musician, pastor and one of the founding leaders of the Vineyard community of churches. Before he passed away in 1997, Wimber authored books on healing and evangelism.

Reprinted by permission: Equipping the Saints

and minister to people, too. He cut his prayer time to three hours a day. Then two.

One day, he said, a young friend who had just spent the morning with God stopped by the house. He had a message from God.

"What did God say?"

"God said, 'Tell Francis I miss him.'"

Who among us, having tasted the sweet intimacy of walking with the Father, does not fear those sad words: "I miss you"?

The Bible emphasizes knowing God intimately, as Father. As Daddy.

Jesus often used agricultural terms. Agriculture, in its most basic sense, is not learning how to control the seasons, soils and processes—it's learning how to cooperate with them.

So it is when you've walked with God. Instead of controlling time, you cooperate with time. Instead of controlling people, you cooperate with them. You love with the love of heaven—for you have been there.

Here's my prayer. You can pray it too:

"Lord, keep me aloft without being aloof. Show me how to remain in orbit with you above Earth's poisoned atmosphere, yet dipping at your command to touch, instruct and heal as Jesus did. May I never again be 'of this world.' May I always—in my own mind and in the oft critical eyes of others—belong to a different kingdom. May I be in the world but not of the world, ministering at your pleasure, marching ever to the sound of the different drummer."
Amen.

—Jamie Buckingham devoted his talents and sacrificed his time to teach and spread the gospel, eventually becoming an internationally renowned author, columnist, and conference speaker. He was a friend to nearly every significant Christian leader in the charismatic movement until his death in 1992 at the age of 59.

Reprinted by permission Charisma Magazine and Strang Communications Company.

into obedience.

There is no sin in seeing the ham and eggs. But if you decide to linger over the ham and eggs, you have just committed breakfast in your heart.

These wrong thoughts are the grenades of the enemy. He hurls them into our minds at the most unexpected and surprising moments. You cannot stop them from coming. But you can develop a habit of capturing them and turning them into opportunities to obey Christ.

THE DICK BUTKUS METHOD

Perhaps until now the temptations have consistently captured you. But as you devote yourself to this discipline you will begin to capture your thoughts. And as you work to capture your thoughts, you'll develop spiritual muscle and character. As far as I can tell there's only one way to do that:

Aggressively attack.

Too many of us have lowered our standards and given ourselves unspoken permission to fail with sexual temptation. We have to make a decision that we will get as aggressive against sin as Dick Butkus got against fullbacks.

Have you ever seen that NFL highlight film on the career of Dick Butkus? Butkus became a living legend because of his aggressiveness. He was unbelievable. He would spit, kick, punch, jab, knee, trip, clothesline, or bite anyone who got in his way.

Why was he so aggressive? Because his objective was to attack the ball-carrier. Butkus didn't just want to tackle the runner, he wanted to remove the guy's helmet with his head still inside. He wanted to cave in the halfback's chest. He wanted to make sure that quarter-

back would never throw another pass in his life.

When you face sexual temptation, you have to turn into a Butkus. This is no time to eat quiche and sip Perrier. There you are, number 51, standing over the center, with steam snorting out of your nostrils. You know that a 240-pound running back of temptation is coming right up the middle with the intention of imprinting his cleat on your chest. As soon as that wrong thought is snapped, you have to step into that hole, take on the 285-pound guard with steroids swimming in his bloodstream, and stuff him while simultaneously clotheslining the back as he tries to get by on your left. You have to capture that wrong thought the same way Butkus would obliterate running backs.

Gentlemen, we must get aggressive toward temptation. We must snort, grunt, and snarl if necessary, but we absolutely cannot be passive. We must adopt an attack mentality.

The next time you are tempted to think illicit sexual thoughts, you must attack. You must get aggressive and hit. When that wrong thought enters your mind, you hit it like Butkus. You capture, seize, gouge and strangle it to the obedience of Christ.

GET ON THE BUS, GUS!

A one-woman man is...

FAITHFUL WITH HIS LIPS.
He doesn't play junior high games with other women. He doesn't kid around about being interested in someone else.

FAITHFUL WITH HIS HANDS.
There's nothing wrong with a hug. But next time you think about hugging a woman, and you're not sure about your motives, don't.

FAITHFUL WITH HIS FEET.
1 Corinthians 6:18 says it flat out: "Flee from sexual immorality." That's how a one-woman man deals with movies, magazines, videos, or any kind of situation that is counterproductive to marriage commitment. He flees.

Someone has said that most men who flee temptation usually have a forwarding address. That won't cut it if you're going to be a one-woman kind of man. Fleeing from immorality means we are willing to

get on the bus, Gus;
make a new plan, Stan;
drop off the key, Lee,
and get yourself free.

—Steve Farrar is the founder and chairman of Men's Leadership Ministries, which has provided a platform for him to speak, write and teach on the subjects that concern men most. Farrar speaks at 25-30 men's conferences a year around the United States and Canada, and he has written some 20 books for men.

Reprinted from Sovereign Grace Ministries (formerly People of Destiny), 7505 Muncaster Mill Rd., Gaithersburg, MD 20877. Used by Permission.

many people are "gun-shy." But the Biblical foundation for relationships is refreshingly simple: "Accept one another, then just as Christ accepted you, in order to bring praise to God" (Ro 15:7).

Unconditional acceptance, offered by the Lord of heaven and earth and demonstrated among God's people, will bring healing and restoration to lives which have been shattered through rejection.

Pride. I've learned (the hard way!) that to experience the full benefit of relationship, we must clothe ourselves with humility. How often God uses our friends to expose our pride! The Bible says, "Better is open rebuke than hidden love. Wounds from a friend can be trusted, but an enemy multiplies kisses" (Pr 27:5-6). We can either choose the road of humility and allow God to use this trustworthy wound for growth in our lives, or we can choose the low road of prideful defensiveness and drift apart.

I've had to make this choice. As Roy and I continued to work out our relationship, painful confrontations arose. One particular time, I became very angry. As I spoke some hurtful words, I saw their impact register in his expression. He grew quiet and did not respond in kind. As I took a deep breath, I felt the Holy Spirit ask me: "Do you have any idea what you are doing?"

I immediately began to apologize and he graciously accepted my apology, but for the next few days I carried the weight of my sin against him. I realized how I had become argumentative with him and how it affected our relationship. As I began to accept responsibility for my reactions, I found a new, softer tone entering into our conversation. I look at that confrontation as a milepost in our friendship.

Convenience. We are a "fast food" culture. Our commitment to convenience characterizes our approach to relationships as well. After hearing a message on relationships, we are disappointed if we don't immediately receive a deep, enduring friendship with at least six people! Relationships take time and great ones are forged over years. There is no "pick-up window" when it comes to friendship!

Ultimately, the type of friendship that I'm describing requires commitment. There may be times when that commitment is all we have, but it will see us through the most difficult situations. I have set this proverb as a personal goal: "A friend loves at all times and a brother is born for adversity" (Pr 17:17).

Roy and I have a real sense of purpose and direction that the Lord has given us. We're learning that the rewards of intimacy far exceed the cost. As we have found grace to respond to the Lord's challenge, we have experienced the great joy of being joined as faithful, committed, and intimate friends. As we encounter each other and learn to love each other unconditionally, we experience the love of God in a more personal way.

FIVE STAGES OF FRIENDSHIP

Stage I: Generality. Our first encounter with someone.
Stage II: Accommodating. Often superficial and generally represents our "public image."
Stage III: Teamwork. Mutual satisfaction in the relationship as more of our external interests and life energy begin to gravitate toward the other individual.
Stage IV: Significant Others. At this point we become vulnerable. We start the process of intimacy by opening up and sharing our innermost thoughts. Quality time and good communication provide a foundation for a relationship in which we take off our masks.
Stage V: Intimacy. We normally relate to one, two, or at most three people at this stage. Often these people are a spouse and one or more best friends with whom we can be open without reservation. Both parties are free, even responsible, to criticize each other when needed and to praise each other without hesitation.

*Not his real name.

—Alan Redrup has served as a pastor of married couples at Covenant Fellowship of Philadelphia. He and his wife, Linda, have four children.

Reprinted from Sovereign Grace Ministries (formerly People of Destiny), 7505 Muncaster Mill Rd., Gaithersburg, MD 20877. Used by Permission.

FULFILLING THE CALL

In 1960, the year my husband, Larry—her youngest son—left for college, Mom and Dad Titus rented their home and began traveling full time so Mom could preach the gospel. Dad recognized the anointing on her life and was willing to be her covering in order to release her calling. She had been faithful to teach in the local church for years; she now was able to take the Word across the land.

Mom loved the home and all it represents. She enjoyed cooking, entertaining, sewing—even ironing, heaven forbid!

But ministry was her life, not a sideline. She left houses, lands and family to fulfill God's call.

She was widowed after 12 years of traveling, but she continued her commitment to preach until God called her home at the age of 81.

Mom Titus has left a legacy not only for her family but for all women who feel a passionate call to ministry. The torch has been passed. Are we motivated to prove ourselves and demand our "rights" in the church, or are we willing to have a servant's heart and sacrifice all for the sake of the gospel?

God is raising up new role models for women in ministry. Like Mom, these women know who they are in Christ.

They will be exalted—quite to their own surprise. For by serving, they will become known.

—Devi Titus, wife of Larry Titus, is among America's most recognized Christian conference speakers and authors. Devi currently serves as the President of Global Pastors' Wives Network. Married for over 49 years, Larry and Devi have two children and multiple grandchildren and great grandchildren. She and her husband travel and speak at conferences extensively worldwide.

called the "weaker vessels" in Scripture that they are the "lesser vessels." While the word used in the text for "weaker vessel" is the Greek word *asthenes*, which means "strengthless," the term is not meant to demean but rather to pay tribute. It is framed in the context that asks men to "(give) honor…as unto the weaker vessel" (1 Peter 3:7).

> "WE MUST ASK THE HARD QUESTIONS. HAVE WE CREATED AN UNFAIR EXEMPTION OF WOMEN FROM THE SAME MERCY AND GRACE THAT WE EXPERIENCE FROM OUR LORD?"

God means for us to bestow upon our wives and sisters in Christ the kind of care one would give to, say, a delicate vase as opposed to a heavy quart jar. The vase, like the jar, is made of glass, but it is weaker and more fragile than the jar. That fragility does not diminish its value; rather, it enhances it.

One of the great wounds that causes our wives and female parishioners to crack and break is our failure to pay attention to their need for special care. While we honor them as "fragile," we must be careful that we do not demean them as "without value."

THROWING STONES

Here is the raw truth: Traces of those men in the Bible who were fully prepared to stone the woman

without recognizing their own culpability can be found within all of us.

How many times in my own life have I been ready to stone my wife for making a mistake that I had made myself? "How could you lock the keys up in the car?" I demand, failing to remember that I have done the same thing in times past.

Double standards that have never been acknowledged become the seedbeds for resentment and frustration. Open confession, it is said, is good for the soul; it may be helpful for marriage and ministry, too.

The worst enemy to the healing of a breach is the denial of its existence. This is a time that we as Christians are learning to take a hard look at the inner crevices of our hearts.

We are suddenly realizing that the potential for sin and injustice exists even in the best of us. We need only study Peter's dream in Acts 10 to see that it is possible to be spiritual on one level and bigoted on another.

My challenge to pastors is to create a climate of dialogue. Show up at women's meetings. Most pastors never minister to the women's groups in their churches; they assign all of that to other women. But I believe it would be mutually gratifying to give some time and attention to "honoring" the women that have done so much to support our visions and ministries.

LEAVING THE CLUB

Some time ago I decided to call the women in our church together during Sunday school just because I noticed that many of them had been bruised and damaged by broken relationships and troubled

pasts. They were very faithful to the church, yet they were wounded, bleeding and in need of God's healing touch.

—I was shocked as I realized that we men tend to have a double standard about how we perceive women who have been marred by sin. We expect them to be so pristine and puritanical. We have denied them the right of being human.

On that day I realized that I had been a member of the "good ol' boys club" for years. That is to say, if a man gets in trouble we like to say to ourselves, "Well, boys will be boys." But if a woman falters in any way, she is perceived as an embarrassment, and a stigma remains.

This form of silent bigotry produces guilt and hinders mercy from reaching those who are spiritually and emotionally broken. So I started teaching the women what Christ says about being whole and healed. Their reaction to that 90-minute time of ministry ended up teaching me.

What started out with 60 women in a Sunday school room in West Virginia grew to fill massive auditoriums. Now we are planning a conference for 50,000 women in New Orleans.

Let us not treat fragile glass vases like quart jars. Our women need to be handled with better care than we have provided in the past.

And as we seek to reach the world for Jesus Christ and minister to those in foreign fields, let's also exercise some caution. We should not be so bent on reaching around the world that we fail to reach the one who has stood by our side all along.

Many, many women in the Bible were healed by the Master just because He took the time to sit by a well, be touched by a need or

roles, the church itself will be male-dominant—and this can lead to issues of control, abuse or sexual sin (the problem of child abuse in the Catholic Church is just one obvious example).

3. **We can't address women's problems without empowering women to address them.** In the 1800s women were not allowed to go to medical school. Some men believed the female brain was smaller than a male's (!), and that women had no business being doctors. What happened when women entered the medical profession? Suddenly there were breakthroughs in medical care, including improvements in gynecology and obstetrics. Women began addressing problems that had been ignored by a male-dominated medical establishment.

Take a look at the world today and you will see millions of girls and women suffering because of sex trafficking, forced child marriage, gang rape, genital mutilation, domestic violence, eating disorders, depression and denial of education. What might happen if we opened the doors wider to empower women in their spiritual gifts? Do women hold a key to solving these problems? I believe we could see social change on an unimaginable scale if we remove gender limitations in ministry.

4. **Women leaders don't hinder men, they help them.** Many Christian men I know seem to fear women's influence. Some gripe about the "feminization" of the church, and they threaten to ban flowers from altars to make the sanctuary look more like a man cave. That's goofy. My Bible says God made flowers as well as antlers and rawhide. He also created women, and He made them to do more than bake cookies and nurse babies. He gave women intelligence, discernment, prophetic insight, gifts of mercy and compassion, leadership abilities and spiritual authority.

When I listen to Abby Olufeyemi preach, or when I see how she shepherds her growing congregation, I receive truth from the Holy Ghost and learn valuable lessons about leadership. She doesn't threaten me; she encourages me. Strong men are not intimidated by gifted women. And strong, gifted women who have Christian character would never try to compete with men or undermine them.

We are all called to be partners and co-heirs in God's kingdom. Let's grow up and embrace biblical equality. †

—J. Lee Grady is the former editor of Charisma and the director of The Mordecai Project (themordecaiproject.org). His latest book is Fearless Daughters of the Bible.

Reprinted by permission: Charisma Magazine and Strang Communications Company.

February 2013, Charisma

parts of the earth, never grows faint or weary? No one can fathom the depths of His understanding. He gives power to the tired and worn out, and strength to the weak" (vv. 28,29 LB). Certainly I could identify with the writer for I was tired and absolutely worn out.

I continued to read: "Even the youths shall be exhausted, and the young men will all give up. But they that wait upon the Lord shall renew their strength. They shall mount up with wings like eagles; they shall run and not be weary; they shall walk and not faint" (vv 30, 31, LB). At that moment it was as though a great infusion of power flooded my very being. I was so excited as I contemplated who God is that I felt I could have thrown my luggage over the building and run to the meeting some miles away.

Suddenly I could not wait to stand before those servants of God and proclaim to them the wonders and majesty, the glory and power, the faithfulness of our great God. Within 30 minutes or so, I did have that privilege, and God empowered and anointed me for the occasion in a marvelous way. Yes, a right understanding of who God is and of all the benefits we enjoy because we belong to Him will revolutionize our lives, launching us into the exciting adventure of supernatural living.

A proper understanding of God's attributes will also open us up to the joy of "delighting in the Lord." In Psalms 37:4 we are promised, "Delight yourself in the Lord; and He will give you the desires of your heart."

How do we "delight" in Him? Psalm 1 gives us some idea of what that means: "Oh the joys of those who do not follow evil men's advice, who do not hang around with sinners, scoffing at the things of God. But"—and note these three things—"they delight in doing everything God wants them to, and day and night are always meditating on His laws and are thinking about ways to follow Him more closely" vv. 1,2 LB).

As the psalm continues, it describes how those who delight in the Lord prosper: "They are like trees along a river bank bearing luscious fruit each season without fail. Their leaves shall never wither, and all they do shall prosper" (v. 3, LB).

The successful, fruitful, joyful Christian life is one that is filled with thoughts focused on our wonderful God and His attributes, getting to know Him better as we seek His face.

What does it mean to "seek God's face?" In 2 Chronicles 7:14 we are admonished through a promise God gave to Solomon: "[If] My people who are called by My name humble themselves and pray, and *seek my face* [italics mine] and turn from their wicked ways, then I will hear from heaven, will forgive their sin, and will heal their land."

For years I have quoted 2 Chronicles 7:14, and my emphasis in using the verse has been on the humbling of ourselves and turning from sin. But once, a minister friend made a passing reference to the phrase, "seeking God's face," and it triggered in my mind some new thoughts about the verse.

The humbling of ourselves and turning from sin are the by-products, or end results, of coming to know our great Creator God as He is, by meditating upon His character and attributes. To seek God's face is to meditate on His sovereignty, His holiness, His power, His wisdom, His love . . . getting to know Him as He is.

The disciples of the first-century church certainly had an exalted view of God. Their God could do anything. There was nothing too great for Him.

The Bible says that the just shall live by faith (Hebrews 10:38). Faith must have an object, and the object of our faith is God. Our view of God determines the quality of our faith. A small view of God results in a small faith. But great faith is the result of a correct, biblical view of God as one who is great and worthy of our trust.

The church today can once again experience the same dynamic of those first believers in Christ, if we, too, become totally absorbed in the character and attributes of our great God. It is then that we will truly begin to believe God for supernatural, impossible things and make an impact for good on the world unlike any time in the history of man.

Adapted from the chapter, "A Supernatural View of God," in the book *Believing God for the Impossible,* by Bill Bright, published by Here's Life Publishers, San Bernardino, Calif.

—Bill Bright was an American evangelist. The founder of Campus Crusade for Christ, he wrote The Four Spiritual Laws in 1952 and produced the Jesus Film in 1979. He died in July of 2003.

Reprinted by permission: Worldwide Challenge

"...Lest that by any means, when I have preached to others, I myself should be a castaway" (I Cor. 9:27)

The second element in Isaiah's vision was a tremendous shock. After looking into the blazing light of God's holiness and seeing who God was, Isaiah suddenly saw himself.

The Western Church has become absolutely blind to this aspect of the great vision. We've lost track of who we are! We think God will accept our view of our sins; that we can negotiate a fresh deal; that we can simply rub out any of the Ten Commandments we don't like. But if we beheld the God of the Book, the mirror of the Gospel before our faces, we would immediately respond as Isaiah did: "Woe is me! I've sinned."

One night a few years ago, as I was preaching at a men's conference, God's presence filled the place. Suddenly, a man in the congregation jumped to his feet and cried, "It's me, it's me, it's me! He's talking about me. It's me!" He walked to the platform, pounded his fist on the platform and cried: "It's me!"

I didn't have to preach anymore. All I had to say was, "Our God is a consuming fire." Hundreds of men came forward, falling on their faces, weeping and crying. One by one they confessed, "I'm cheating in business...I've stolen tools from the garage where I work." Two hours later, they returned to their chairs, minus the filth that had accumulated in their lives. It had been carved off by the hand of Almighty God. I've seldom seen a moment of such glory. And all because one man said, "I'm unclean. And I'm among a people of unclean lips." His words broke us all. It takes only one man to say, "I have sinned," for revival to begin.

Once Isaiah had spoken those words, an angel came. He had in his hands a live coal, taken from the altar with tongs. The altar of God is so holy, that even a sinless angel dares not touch it with his hands. After the coal touched Isaiah's lips, he was not the same man. No longer was he overcome with the holiness of God: he had experienced a purifying touch from the altar of God.

In the third aspect of this vision, Isaiah hears the heart of God. The Lord asks, "Oh, who will go for Us? Whom shall I send?" Isaiah feels God's pain for those who need to hear the glorious Gospel of salvation by grace through faith. The religion of a hundred million Japanese workaholics is not Shintoism or Buddhism, but the yen. They long to know that there is a God who loves them. Seven hundred fifty million Indian Hindus have never heard the name of Jesus. They live in bondage and fear to 350,000 demonic gods and goddesses, waiting to be touched with the radiant Gospel of Jesus Christ.

God's waiting for somebody who's been touched by the coal from the altar to eavesdrop on heaven and respond as Isaiah did: "Here am I, send me." The Hebrew actually says, "Look me over, Lord, and see if I'll do. Is there any possible way You could use me?" This is the humility of a man who, having seen the holiness of God and having reckoned with his own sin, has experienced the sanctifying grace of God. If arrogance and presumption have crept into your relationship with God, get on your face before God and pray, "God have mercy. I have lost sight of your holiness." Let God's angel retrieve a live coal from the altar of His grace and burn your sin away.

Then recline on Jesus' breast until you hear a voice from heaven say, "Whom shall I send? And who will go for Us?" If you hear that voice, respond, "Oh, God, is there any way you can use me?"

Adapted from a message given at the Full Gospel Business Men's Fellowship International convention in Orlando, Florida.

—Mark Rutland is a missionary, evangelist, ordained minister of the International Ministerial Fellowship, former president of Oral Roberts University and now part of the preaching team at Jentezen Franklin's Free Gospel Church in Atlanta, Georgia.

Reprinted by permission: Christ for the Nations CFNI, P.O. Box 769000, Dallas, TX 75376-9000, 800-933-2364

we can also make a person sick with negative words. I've seen verbally abused children vomit because of the abuse they experienced.

Three students at Dallas Theological Seminary conspired to play a trick on a fellow student, John. They had this planned ahead of time. As John went to his first class, one of the students walked up to him and said, "John, you don't look very well today." John said, "What do you mean? I feel great. I had a good night of rest." "Well, I just don't think you look well today."

The bell rang, and John went to class. On his way to his second class, the next student came up and said, "John, you really don't look very well." And John said, "You know, I really don't feel very well."

Then between the second and the third class, the third student came up and said, "John, you really look sick." He said, "I am. I'm going to go home and go to bed." That illustration proves the power of our words. John became sick as he listened to others telling him he looked sick. Obviously, we can use words for good or for bad.

Christians need to learn how to use words for good. Of all people, God's children ought to know how to use pleasant words. Remember that "pleasant words are like a honeycomb, sweetness to the soul and health to the bones." We need to remember others in our ministry, in our business and in our home.

"A word fitly spoken (spoken in the right context, in the right situation and in the right way) is like apples of gold in settings of silver" (Prov. 25:11). It's the way we use words that makes all the difference. There are words—good and bad—that we never forget. We can all think of some words that were spoken to us that we have never forgotten.

My mind goes back to when I was 6 years old and in the first grade. My teacher, Olive Owens, wrote one word on the chalkboard. It was a word I'd never seen before. She wrote it in beautiful cursive handwriting. The word was "me."

She said, "now boys and girls, what I would like for you to do is to write the word 'me.'" I picked up my pencil and began writing on the yellow pad on my desk. I looked at the word on the chalkboard, and then I looked at my paper. I tried to get my hand to move and copy the word in cursive. It was terribly hard.

Then the teacher started around the classroom, looking at every child's paper, then patting them on the back. Finally, she started down my row. By that time, my heart was just about ready to drop right through the floor. I looked at my paper; that word looked more like a runaway seismograph than the word "me." I was scared to death.

As the teacher stopped at my desk, the anxiety in my soul had risen so high that I burst into tears. She looked at my paper, and she looked at me. Seeing my anxiety, she leaned over and in a very soft and quiet voice said, "That's okay, Gene." That's all she said.

Then she bent down and gently kissed me on the cheek before she went on to the next student. Do you think that made a difference in my life, in my attitude toward school or toward that teacher? You better believe it did! One time in the second grade, Ms. Owens had to spank me because I kicked off my shoes in the snow. I remember how proud I was to be spanked by that teacher! She was my favorite. Her kindness even made a difference in my attitude toward receiving discipline from her.

There is tremendous power in words. Some of our words will never be forgotten. The power of words lies in the emotion behind them. Our words, whether encouraging or rebuking, will mean nothing unless people know we love them. But when people know we love them, it's amazing how they respond to what we say.

The Apostle Paul culminated a beautiful passage of Scripture about the Second Coming of Christ by saying, "Comfort one another with these words" (1 Thes. 4:18). We can encourage one another with the Word of God.

God uses logos (words) to demonstrate, to illustrate and to communicate Jesus Christ, the Living *Word.* May God help us to utter words that are aptly spoken, words that bring pleasant memories, words that bring healing to the soul and to the bones—the physical being—of others!

Adapted from a message given at CFNI-Dallas.

—Gene A. Getz is a college and seminary professor, writer and pastor who successfully integrated the philosophy of renewal into a local church setting. His best known text, Sharpening the Focus of the Church, looks at the church through the lenses of Scripture, history and culture. Many of his books focus on developing local church leaders and Christian character.

Reprinted by permission: Christ for the Nations
CFNI, P.O. Box 769000, Dallas, TX 75376-9000, 800-933-2364

circumstances expose what is truly in one's heart.

GOD TESTS YOUR COMMITMENT

God wants to know whether or not you will keep His commandments under any and all circumstances. He must know if you will follow Him, even under pressure—pressure caused by grievances, injustices, temptations, blunders, misunderstandings, or a host of other reasons. Will you choose to obey the Lord even if it is difficult; or will you follow the path of least, resistance?

The wilderness experience is not meant to make your life miserable but to reveal whether or not you can handle all that God is planning for you. The purpose of this test is to stretch you and to enlarge your borders for greater usefulness in the kingdom of God. Wilderness experiences are actually opportunities!

Wilderness experiences teach biblical principles and expose internal problems so they can be purged and help prepare you for the blessings and ministry God has planned for your life. One of the basic pitfalls of the wilderness experience is that one is seldom aware of the connection between the promises of God and the fulfillment of God's promises. In between the promise and the fulfillment is a "wilderness" or test to teach and to prepare you.

THE ISAAC TEST

Now we come to the test which is not always in the Bible school counseling manual—the test which supposedly was only for Abraham. This is what I call the "Isaac Test": a trial which may shake the very depths of your religious preconceptions; for it may not involve the negative aspects of your life but a positive area—one that perhaps came from the very hand of God.

One day Abraham found himself being asked to give up the very gift that God had given him—Isaac. This blessed son who had been promised of God and was so long in coming. The son who represented much pleasure, joy, and happiness in his parents' lives. Isaac embodied his father's future, security and heritage. Abraham had poured his life—his time, money, energy, love and affection—into this legitimate gift from God. Now, God wanted it back.

WHY WOULD GOD IMPOSE
SUCH A REQUEST?

Such an entreaty by God is for the purpose of

testing our faith and obedience, because God desires to bless in an even greater way. Learning the art of giving up is difficult, but it always results in becoming more like Christ and receiving better things from God. This principle is illustrated over and over in the Bible: Daniel gave up the king's food, Hannah gave up Samuel, Jochebed gave up Moses, the young lad gave up his loaves and fishes, Paul gave up privacy, sleep, reputation, etc., and Jesus gave up heaven.

My "Isaac" was an area of my life which likewise had been given to me by God. I had literally poured thousands of hours, enormous amounts of energy, and sacrificed finances to help my Isaac grow and mature. It had captured my love and affection, because it had given me so much fulfillment and satisfaction over the years. Then one day I inwardly heard a still, small voice saying, "Dennis, give mc your Isaac; and I will bless you in an even greater way."

As soon as I recognized the Voice to be the Holy Spirit, I began to seek God further regarding the meaning of this. What was my Isaac? I had already surrendered my life, my wife and three children, my possessions. What could it be?

Since my return to Christ For The Nations in 1973 after several years of missionary work with Youth With A Mission, under the direction of the Holy Spirit, I had been developing and teaching Bible courses. As I taught year after year, my spiritual rewards, fulfillment and satisfaction were tremendous. Then, two years ago the board of Christ For The Nations elected me as President of the organization. I accepted the position as an open door from the Lord. But as time passed, I began to experience fatigue and frustration. My teaching, which meant so much to me, was taking a backseat to my newly-acquired duties and responsibilities. I had been thrust into this new calling which demanded so much of my time and diligence. Clearly I was in a wilderness experience, and God was dealing with me about my Isaac.

MY "ISAAC" IDENTIFIED

As I sought the Lord concerning the identity of my Isaac, I was startled at what He showed me. My Isaac was something I had never imagined it could be: *my teaching ministry.* When I realized what God was asking of me, I struggled for a time. But I knew that if I was going to continue to grow in God, there was only one possible choice—obedience!

When I finally identified the Isaac and made the decision to do as God had asked, I experienced a fresh release of God's Spirit; and a new awareness of His love and power enveloped my soul. As a result of

fruits" (II Tim. 2:6). I needed the Word to become life to me before I could impart it.

Later, while pastoring a church in Oakland, California, my dear parishioners requested that I do a verse by verse study of Genesis. Oh, the days of creation were thrilling. And walking with the patriarchs was wonderful. But suddenly, before I realized it, we had arrived at chapter 22. At 11:00 p.m. the night before I was to preach, I still had no sermon.

I approached the everlasting Author of Genesis 22. "And He (God) said, Take now thy son, thine only son Isaac, whom thou lovest, and get thee unto the land of Moriah; and offer him there for a burnt offering..." (Gen. 22:2).

Did Abraham consult his servant, Eliezer? Scripture says, "...In the multitude of counselors there is safety" (Prov. 11:14). Abraham was about to go through the greatest trial of his life. But perhaps the patriarch anticipated his faithful servant responding, "Father Abraham, are you sure *God* spoke to you? Your God has never put anyone to such a test. There's no precedent for this."

Neither does the Word record Abraham bidding Sarah goodbye, though he was preparing to be gone four days. If he had told his wife the nature of his excursion, surely she would have objected, "Don't you *dare* touch a hair of his head! He belongs as much to me as to you." Had she no right to protest?

There come times in our lives, in our service, in our relationships with God, when He deals with us uniquely. We can go to no one for counsel. No one will truly understand; no one has been there. At such times we must walk in close communion with God, depending on His Word alone.

God had spoken, not to Eliezer or Sarah, but to Abraham. He had to obey God, regardless of

what others thought. One key to being blessed by God is to be deaf to every human voice and alert to God's.

Abraham obeyed quickly. The Bible doesn't record Abraham weeping as he ascended the mount. What gave the man such assurance, such confidence, such peace, such faith? As I read this next verse, a truth was revealed to me which totally liberated my wife and me from the duty and hurt of a sacrificial life. At the foot of Mount Moriah, Abraham turned to his servants and said, "Abide ye here...I and the lad will go yonder and *worship*..." (Gen. 22:5). Abraham went up the mountain not to sacrifice, but to do something higher, something much more spiritual: he went to worship.

What's the difference between worship and sacrifice? In sacrifice, we have our eyes on what we're giving to God, and we hold on to it until the last moment. In worship, we have our eyes on God; whatever He requires, we yield willingly.

Job was the greatest man in all the East. He had more cattle, more herds, more flocks than anyone else. He had a huge retinue of servants, a small army of soldiers, seven sons and three daughters. But one day, he lost everything. Thieves stole his herds, flocks and camels; these men also murdered his servants. His sons and daughters were killed while attending a banquet in the eldest son's home. Then Job himself contracted an awful disease, and his skin began erupting in sores. In the midst of all this, his wife turned on him, advising him to curse God and die. And then there were Job's friends—three practicing psychiatrists under the guise of "comforters." Job was completely devastated.

What did Job do? He fell on the ground and worshiped. How could anyone worship, at a time like that? His heart was broken with grief, and he had become a pauper

overnight. But Job's eye was on God. We are plagued with fear and unbelief when we look at our problems and our burdens—the seeming impossibilities we face. Our faith is challenged and begins to crumble. We must lift up our eyes and look to Jesus—the Author and Finisher of our faith—and worship Him.

I have known believers who have walked away from God because a loved one died or because a believer lost his job. They blame God for everything. But a worshiper triumphs through anything—be it opposition, deprivation, pain, loneliness, sickness.

Worship demands two things: extravagant love and absolute surrender. "Take now thy *son...whom thou lovest...and offer* him there for a burnt offering." It is no wonder that in verse 17 God responds to Abraham, "You have proved that you love Me more than you love your son. I'm going to bless you and bless you and bless you..."

Our trials will become either acts of sacrifice or acts of worship. If we choose to worship, we'll never have the pain of sacrifice. As we look upon Him, we'll see His worthiness.

Are you battling the flesh? Is it a duty to obey the word of the Lord? "Turn your eyes upon Jesus, Look full in His wonderful face, And the things of earth will grow strangely dim, in the light of His glory and grace."

Adapted from a message given at CFNI, Dallas, Texas

— Paul Schoch is a long-time pastor, speaker and conference organizer, who for many years pastored what is now Sequoyah Community Church, Assemblies of God, in Oakland, California.

Reprinted by permission: Christ for the Nations CFNI, P.O. Box 769000, Dallas, TX 75376-9000, 800-933-2364

Satan makes his strongest accusations. For example, I receive probably five invitations to speak for each one I am able to accept. Invariably, once I accept an invitation, I begin wondering if I should have taken any of the other four. If I decide to go to a small, poorer church because they probably really need me, but can't afford me, I can become self-righteous and smug. Yet if I choose to go to a larger church, I feel condemned because I know they will pay me well.

No matter what we do in ministry, there is always a reasonable doubt we are ministering for righteous reasons. Even if we happen to do something totally unselfish, we tend to become self-righteous about it! As a result, there will always be one who stands at our right hand calling out, "Defiled! Unclean!" Satan loves to point out every spot of impurity and magnify it. What we must learn then, is how to handle his accusations, especially when we are "guilty as charged."

WHAT WE ARE TARNISHES
WHAT WE DO

The accusation against Joshua was not that he was dirty, but that his garments were. Sadly enough, even the very garments for service, our ministerial robes, callings, or anointings, become defiled because they are on us. What we are tarnishes what we do.

As already stated, it is rare that any gift of the Spirit functions through us purely. Something of our fleshly nature usually gets involved. If it is a vocal gift in operation, we tend to embellish the message a little. Perhaps we don't do it consciously, but by our thinking and wording, we change some of what is meant. Occasionally we might not even let God say what He wants to say because we don't really believe it. Other times we may color what we feel we have received from God to make it a bit more interesting or palatable. What is remarkable though, is that God knew we would do this when He entrusted us with the gifts. While we choose to think of "our" gifts as totally spiritual and godly functions, the Lord God sees the workings of our flesh in the midst of them. Fortunately, God can override us and work around our meddling. Our flesh doesn't disturb God as much as we would suppose. What it does do, however, is give our enemy a basis for accusation.

As believers, we come into the presence of God feeling somewhat acceptable, usually having compared ourselves with other people. But before we begin to worship the devil points to us and says, "Unclean! Throw him (or her) out!" In substantiation he adds some statements like "Remember, God, that sermon on Sunday? It was filthy! It was only his way of lashing out at the church board," or "Remember when that gift of the Spirit operated through him? It wasn't totally pure. It was mostly what had been heard in the counseling chambers." Such accusations indeed have truth in them. The defilement is real, and Satan's demand that God cast us out of His presence stems from his own experience.

But because of the work of Christ at Calvary, God has another way of dealing with our defilement. Although He is aware of our uncleanness, He chooses to cast away the soiled garments rather than the person who wears them. Joshua was not condemned; he was stripped and reclothed with the garment of Christ's righteousness. The change was not effected by the priest; he was merely asked to surrender the old and accept the new.

Similarly, the change that is needed in order for us to stand in God's presence can not be accomplished by us. Only God can make us pure in His sight. His greatest problem, however, is in getting permission to remove our ministerial robes from us. Few things are more threatening to us than to have God remove what he has given. Too often, in our ignorance, we argue: "But God, this is my calling. This is 'my ministry.' I've spent my entire life working at this." Vainly we try to defend ourselves; because we don't understand that it is not us that God has difficulties with. We have already been "accepted in the Beloved" (Ephesians 1:6). But it is our garments of service that gives cause for the accusations against us. That's where the uncleanness is seen.

OUR PROBLEM IS WE HAVE NOT
LEARNED TO SEPARATE OUR GIFTS
FROM OUR PERSON.

Our problem is that we haven't learned how to separate our gifts from our person. Yet God can and does. He wants us to learn that we are not "the ministry" we perform. The ministry is temporal; the person is eternal.

So often we hide our true selves from each other by wearing every garment of righteousness we have. Fearing to be transparent to others, we empty our closet instead, putting on everything we have in order to impress people. By these garments we proclaim, "I'm

day of my life to date, so far as giving my day in complete and continual surrender to God is concerned ... I remember how as I looked at people with a love God gave, they looked back and acted as though they wanted to go with me. I felt then that for a day I saw a little of that marvelous pull that Jesus had as He walked along the road day after day, "God-intoxicated" and radiant with the endless communion of His soul with God.

What do you think of Laubach's adventure? How would you answer his questions? *Can we have that contact with God all the time? All the time awake, fall asleep in His arms, and awaken in His presence?*

Is such a goal realistic? Or do you think the idea of constant fellowship with God is somewhat fanatical, even extreme? Whatever your opinion may be of Laubach's adventure, you have to agree with one of his observations about Jesus. He enjoyed unbroken communion with God. And if we're to be just like Jesus, you and I will strive to do the same.

GOD'S TRANSLATOR

Jesus' relationship with God went far deeper than a daily appointment. Our Savior was always aware of His Father's presence. Listen to His words:

The Son can do nothing on his own, but only what he sees the Father doing; for whatever the Father does, the Son does likewise.

—Jn. 5:19, NRSV

I do nothing on my own. As I hear, I judge.

—Jn. 5:30, NRSV

I am in the Father and the Father is in me.

—Jn. 14:11, NRSV

Clearly, Jesus didn't act unless He saw His Father act. He didn't judge until He heard His Father judge. No act or deed occurred without the guidance of His Father. His words have the ring of a translator.

There were a few occasions in Brazil when I served as a translator for an English speaker. He stood before the audience, complete with the message. I stood at his side, equipped with the language. My job was to convey his story to the listeners. I did my best to allow his words to come through me. I was not at liberty to embellish or subtract. When the speaker gestured, I gestured. As his volume increased, so did mine. When he got quiet, I did, too.

When He walked this earth, Jesus was "translating" God all the time. When God got louder, He got louder. When God gestured, Jesus gestured. He was so in sync with the Father that He could declare, "I am in the Father and the Father is in me" (Jn. 14:11, NRSV). It was as if He heard a voice others were missing.

Because Jesus could hear what others couldn't, He acted differently than they did. Remember when everyone was troubled about the man born blind? Jesus wasn't. Somehow He knew that the blindness would reveal God's power (see Jn. 9:3). Remember when everyone was distraught about Lazarus' illness? Jesus wasn't. Rather than hurry to His friend's bedside, he said, "This sickness will not end in death. It is for the glory of God, to bring glory to the Son of God" (Jn. 11:4, NCV). It was as if Jesus could hear what no one else could. How could a relationship be more intimate? Jesus had unbroken communion with His Father.

Do you suppose He desires the same for us? Absolutely. Paul says we have been "predestined to be conformed to the image of his Son" (Ro. 8:29, NRSV). Let me remind you: God loves you just the way you are, but He refuses to leave you that way. He wants you to be just like Jesus. God desires the same abiding intimacy with us that He has with His Son.

PICTURES OF INTIMACY

God draws several pictures to describe the relationship He envisions. One is of a vine and a branch.

"I am the vine, and you are the branches. If any remain in me and I remain in them, they produce much fruit. But without me they can do nothing ... If you remain in me and follow my teachings, you can ask anything you want, and it will be given to you"

—Jn. 15:5, 7, NCV

God wants to be as close to us as a branch is to a vine. One is an extension of the other. It's impossible to tell where one starts and the other ends. The branch isn't connected to the vine only at the moment of bearing fruit. The gardener doesn't keep the branches in a box and then, on the day he wants grapes, glue them to the vine. No, the branch constantly draws nutrition from the vine. Separation means certain death.

God also uses the temple to depict the intimacy He desires. "Don't you know," Paul writes, "that your body is the temple of the Holy Spirit, who lives in you and who was given to you by God?" (1 Cor. 6:19, TEV). Think with me about the temple for a moment.

shepherd. How can I grow familiar with the voice of God? Here are a few ideas.

Give God your waking thoughts. Before you face the day, face your Father. Before you step out of bed, step into His presence. I have a friend who makes it a habit to roll out of his bed onto his knees and begin his day in prayer. Personally, I don't get that far. With my head still on the pillow and my eyes still closed, I offer God the first seconds of my day. The prayer is not lengthy and far from formal. Depending on how much sleep I got, it may not even be intelligible, often nothing more than, "Thank You for a night's rest. I belong to You today."

C. S. Lewis wrote these words:

The moment you wake up each morning ... [all] your wishes and hopes for the day rush at you like wild animals. And the first job of each morning consists in shoving them all back; in listening to that other voice; taking that other point of view; letting that other, larger, stronger, quieter life come flowing in.

Here is how the psalmist began his day: "Every morning I tell you what I need and I wait for your answer" (Ps. 5:3, NCV). Which leads to the second idea:

Give God your waiting thoughts. Spend time with Him in silence. The mature married couple has learned the treasure of shared silence; they don't need to fill the air with constant chatter. Just being together is sufficient. Try being silent with God. "Be still, and know that I am God" (Ps. 46:10). Awareness of God is a fruit of stillness before God.

Give God your whispering thoughts. Through the centuries Christians have learned the value of brief sentence prayers, prayers that can be whispered anywhere in any setting. Laubach sought to stay in communion with God by asking Him questions. Every two or three minutes he would ask, "Am I in Your will, Lord? Am I pleasing You, Lord?"

Imagine considering every moment as a potential time of communion with God. By the time your life is over, you will have spent six months at stoplights, eight months opening junk mail, a year and a half looking for lost stuff (double that number in my case), and a whopping five years standing in various lines. Why don't you give these moments to God? By giving God your whispering thoughts, the common becomes uncommon. Simple phrases such as "Thank you, Father," "Be sovereign in this hour, O Lord," "You are my resting place, Jesus" can turn a commute into a pilgrimage. You needn't leave your office or kneel in your kitchen. Just pray where you are. Let the kitchen become a cathedral or the classroom a chapel. Give God your whispering thoughts.

Give God your waning thoughts. At the end of the day, let your mind settle on Him. Conclude the day as you began it: talking to God. Thank Him for the good parts. Question Him about the hard parts. See His mercy. Seek His strength, and as you close your eyes, take assurance in the promise: "He who watches over Israel will neither slumber nor sleep" (Ps. 121:4). If you fall asleep as you pray, don't worry. What better place to doze off than in the arms of your Father?

This article was excerpted from Max Lucado's book Just Like Jesus, published by Thomas Nelson.

Used by permission of Thomas Nelson.

—Max Lucado is the author of more than 50 books, including In the Grip of Grace and When God Whispers Your Name (both Word). Max served for 20 years as the Senior Minister of the Oak Hills Church of Christ in San Antonio, Texas. He says his greatest accomplishment is finding a one-in-a-million wife and having three unbelievable daughters.

iquity and holes and dives where men hide from the light because of the sin and evil that is upon them. There was a day when I saw demons cry out at the very presence of the power of God that rested.

Then I went back to my secret place broken. I said, "God, I have asked Thee for all that I desire and still my heart is not satisfied. Nor do I feel that I have touched the thing that Thou has called me to. In my youth I had expended myself with all the things that my heart had desired."

Then one more time a gracious and loving God visited me in the night season. He said, "Now, what is it that thou dost desire?" In brokenness of heart, I bowed before Him and I said, "God, only that thing which Thou dost desire to give unto me."

He came unto me and said, "Come with Me and I will take you on a journey." He took me past my friends. He took me past those with whom I had come into the house of the Lord. He took me into a desolate place. He caused me to go into a place alone in the wilderness. I said, "Oh my God, Thou has cut me off from those I love. What art Thou doing unto me?" He said, "I take thee to the place where all men must come if their heat's cry is to be fulfilled."

At a certain hour, I bowed before a gate that is called, "The Eye of the Needle." There before the eye of the needle I heard the voice of the Lord say, "Bow low." I bowed low. He said, "No, lower." So I bowed lower. He said, "Yet lower. Thou dost not go low enough." So I went as low as I could go.

I had upon my back my books of learning. I had with me my instruments of music. I had with me my gifts and abilities. He said unto me, "Thou hast too

much, thou canst not go through this gate." I said, "God, Thou has given me these books. Thou hast given me these abilities." He said, "Drop them, or thou dost not go." So I dropped them. I went through a very small gate that is called "the eye of the needle." As I went through this gate, I heard the voice of the Lord say, "Now rise to the others side." As I rose, a very strange thing happened to me. For lo, the gate which was so small that I must lay aside everything was so wide I could not fill it. As I stood in the presence of the Lord I said, "God, what is this thing that Thou hast done unto me for my soul is now satisfied?"

He said, "Thou hast come through the gate of worship. Now come up to the circle of the earth and I will show thee a great mystery. I will reveal unto thee the thing that I am doing among the sons of men." The Spirit of the Lord caught me away. He took me to the circle of the earth, higher than the eagle flies, beyond where the clouds can rumble, beyond where the sun shines or the moon finds her path. There at the throne of my God, He said, "Look down upon My people."

I saw strange things. I saw my companions gathered around a very small gate. I saw them wringing their hands and crying. They were saying to one another, "God hath given us these instruments of war. This sword is my sword and I will work with the enemy. I will bring the enemy down. I cannot go through this gate, for, if I go through this gate, I must put down my sword. God has called me to be a warrior and therefore, I will not do it."

And I heard another one say, "Me? Lay down my instruments of music? Lay down all that God has given unto me, just to go

through that silly little gate, to be nothing but a bare man who comes out on the other side stripped of everything? I cannot do this thing!" I saw them as they stood aside in their pride, afraid to bow themselves before a very small gate. Then I saw again, as the Lord brought me closer to the gate, I saw a man bow low, laying down everything that he had. As he came through the very wide gate on the other side, his instruments of music were there. His sword was there. His books were there. The power was there.

The Word of the Lord came to me, "Go now and tell this people before you, I have given unto this people extreme talents and much ability. I have called you who are instrumentalists to play. But I say unto you this night, if you do not come through the very small gate, which is the gate of worship, and bow low and lay before Me thine instruments, thy talents, thy abilities, thy vision and thy power, thou shalt always be among those who will only be able to minister to the hearts of men and bless the hearts of men. But there is a gate open in the Church in this hour which is a very small gate. Through that gate only men who are worshippers will go. These men will lay their talents before their God. These men will say, 'God, we will be worshippers.' Through that wide gate they will come. As they come through that wide gate—hear again the Word of the Lord—they will arise again on the other side, not to minister unto men, but to minister unto their God.

"I have brought this people together this night to make unto you a choice. You can minister unto men and I will cause you to sway the hearts of men with your talent. Or, you can go through a very small gate and while making new worshippers, you will minister

savoring every word, letting herself be saturated by His presence. Jesus pointed to Mary's example. "Come and sit, Martha," He urged. "Not only for a moment, not only for an hour. Never mind the groaning of our stomachs. Sit here and soak in My presence until your soul stops grumbling" (see Lk. 10:41-42).

Although I love the camaraderie of teamwork with Jesus, I also need an undistracted time just to look into His face. Jesus pursues more than a business relationship with me. He also wants to spend time together talking. He invites me to linger. To pull up a cushion and sit a spell. To be still and know that He is God.

Jesus has pursued me for more than a relationship with Him. He also shows me the way to communion with His Father.

One day Jesus led Peter, James, and John up on a mountain to pray. Unknown to them, they were being included in a sacred fellowship between Jesus and His Father. When it finally sank in, Peter blurted, "This is great! Let's build temples where we can come back to worship again" (see Lk. 9:33).

The Father's voice resounded from the clouds, "This is my Son, whom I have chosen; listen to him" (v. 35). God was telling Peter that there was no need to climb a special mountain to worship the Father. In Jesus he also had the presence of the Father. Look at Him. Listen to Him.

Many times I'm also in a thick fog when Jesus calls me to fellowship. I am slow to realize the awesome privilege of the invitation (especially when it comes at dawn). But as I sit in a silent house with the Word of God open on my lap, the comforting familiarity of my Companion gives me courage to boldly approach God's throne. On Jesus' arm I am just as welcome in the Royal Family as He is.

CALLED TO BATTLE

As surely as there is time for quiet rest, there comes a time for action. Companions encounter a variety of experiences if the road is at all long. Perhaps the greatest honor of being Christ's companion is when He calls us to assist Him in battle.

When Jesus set out toward Gethsemane, He invited the disciples to accompany Him. At the midpoint, He allowed only His most trusted soldiers to continue with Him. Peter, James, and John had proven their loyalty. He trusted them to support Him and fight by His side against His spiritual opponent.

I have been awakened at night with a sense of urgency to pray against the forces of evil. With no idea who or what is in jeopardy. I acknowledge the holiness of God and the power of Christ's blood. I am honored to be summoned by the One who fought for me. I feel privileged to stand shoulder to shoulder with Him. And brandishing the sword of the Spirit against the accuser I have felt sin collapse with a relief in my soul.

I love the loving heart of Jesus that has called me to His side. There is no greater experience than that of His presence. There is no greater honor than to be His friend. And there is no greater joy than to serve the One who graciously chose me to be on His team. I love Him for pursuing me until I followed Him.

—Sandy Clark writes, proofreads, serves on a worship team, is a soloist, and organizes church events and craft shows.

Used by permission from Sandy Clark.

KNOWING COURSES

How To Know God's Voice—In Intimate Friendship

Intimate Friendship with God! Can we experience such a relationship with the Creator of the universe? Here we examine what the Bible teaches us about the fear of the Lord, and how we can, indeed, have a deeper, more intimate relationship with Him. This is a very personal, yet freeing course on growing intimacy with God.

How To Know God's Voice—In Worship

The focus of this course is on ministering to the Lord. During our time together the Lord draws us corporately into His presence as we worship Him. We study what worship is, why we worship, and how we worship.

How To Know God's Voice—In His Presence

The Lord is calling each one of His sheep to come into His presence and to know Him in a deeper way. This course is not for the new believer nor the faint in heart. Those who are serious about knowing the Father in a more intimate way will find this course challenging but rewarding. Examining Jesus' last days on earth will direct us into the presence of the Lord. This course is for those who have completed other ZOE courses.

How To Know God's Voice—In the Coming of the Lord

Many are proclaiming dates and times when the Lord Jesus will return for His bride. This course is designed to focus on our preparation for His coming, not when He is coming, and to better understand the Lord's statement of Revelation 22:20: "Yes, I am coming." It is the goal of this course to prepare ourselves as the bride of Christ, with hearts that will respond with "Amen. Come, Lord Jesus."

FOLLOWING COURSES

How To Follow God's Voice—In Healing

During this course we examine the scriptures in which Jesus healed the sick. The Holy Spirit highlights these passages as we study, and our faith increases! We realize that Jesus is the Healer, and we are simply His vessels as we listen to and follow His voice.

How To Follow God's Voice—In Power

Evangelism is often thought of as a bad word! In this course we come to realize that God has a special plan for evangelism for us if we are only sensitive and obedient to His voice. Preparing your testimony, leading someone in salvation, and discipling others are a few of the topics discussed in this course. This is a real life-changer as we minister in "power evangelism!"